_10_   **DATE DUE**

Updated Edition!

COLLEGE
PLANNING

for Gifted
Students

Updated Edition!

COLLEGE PLANNING

Choosing and Getting Into
the Right College

for Gifted
Students

Sandra L. Berger

PRUFROCK PRESS INC.
WACO, TEXAS

Library of Congress Cataloging-in-Publication Data

Berger, Sandra L.
 College planning for gifted students : choosing and getting into the right college / by
Sandra L. Berger. -- Updated edition.
     pages cm
 Includes bibliographical references.
 ISBN 978-1-61821-147-7 (pbk.)
 1. College choice--United States. 2. Gifted children--Education--United States. 3.
College student orientation--United States. I. Title.
 LB2350.5.B47 2014
 378.1'98--dc23
                              2013046953

Edited by Bethany Johnsen

Cover design by Raquel Trevino and layout design by Allegra Denbo

ISBN-13: 978-1-61821-147-7

Printed in the United States of America.

At the time of this book's publication, all facts and figures cited are the most current
available. All telephone numbers, addresses, and website URLs are accurate and active. All
publications, organizations, websites, and other resources exist as described in the book,
and all have been verified. The author and Prufrock Press Inc. make no warranty or guar-
antee concerning the information and materials given out by organizations or content
found at websites, and we are not responsible for any changes that occur after this book's
publication. If you find an error, please contact Prufrock Press Inc.

Prufrock Press Inc.
P.O. Box 8813
Waco, TX 76714-8813
Phone: (800) 998-2208
Fax: (800) 240-0333
http://www.prufrock.com

To my daughters, Bonnie, Judy, and Deb, my husband and 5 grandchildren, who inspired this book. It's almost time for the next generation to look at colleges.

TABLE OF CONTENTS

Acknowledgements

College Planning for Gifted Students, written by a parent and longtime advocate for gifted children, is the product of many efforts. Numerous administrators, counselors, teachers, parents, and students were interviewed for and contributed to this book. I express sincere appreciation to the individuals listed below and to the many students and adults who, over the years, contributed indirectly by speaking freely about their concerns and experiences. Last, but certainly not least, I very much appreciate the efforts of the energetic and creative people at Prufrock Press. Special thanks goes to my friend Dorothy Knopper, Open Space Communications, who read early versions and made helpful suggestions.

I would like to thank the following contributors:

» The parent of a learning-disabled child and a former homeschool student for telling their stories.

» The section on career centers was prepared with the assistance of Laurie Kobick, who was the College/Career Center Resource Specialist at Thomas Jefferson High School for Science and Technology in Fairfax, VA.

» Guidelines for a teacher recommendation were contributed by Bernis von zur Muehlen of James Madison High School, Fairfax County Public Schools in Virginia.

» Guidelines for writing a college application essay were contributed by Gail Hubbard of Prince William County Public Schools in Manassas, VA.

» The section on college costs was contributed by Joseph Re, Executive Vice President of Octameron Associates in Alexandria, VA.

» The student questionnaire Why Are You Going to College? (p. 57) and the questions students may want to ask during the college interview (p. 167) were based on the work of an independent college counselor.

COLLEGE PLANNING

College planning is a major event in the lives of many families. Some parents dress their infants in tiny clothing bearing their alma mater's colors and mascots, certain that someday, their child will follow in their footsteps. Other families claim to "bleed" maroon, burnt orange, navy blue and gold, or crimson red, with generations of family members attending the same university. Smartphones are enclosed in a case bearing the logo of the owner's alma mater. Across the nation, longtime rivalries are upheld during football and basketball season and carried over to friendly game day disputes between siblings, friends, or neighbors who chose to attend competing universities. Only in America is the decal from almost any college displayed proudly on the rear window of the family car.

The hopes and dreams of many American families are connected to a college education. We are surrounded by reminders of higher education—everything from ads for college financing to slick TV descriptions of the competing universities during halftime at the fall football games. In the 21st century, attending college is part of the American success story.

High school students and their parents often have strong feelings about attending or not attending college, but once the decision is made to go, choosing the *right* college becomes a different matter altogether. The path from secondary to higher education is poorly marked. Students surveyed for this book said that trying to select a college is confusing, because there is no sound basis for making a decision. They felt overwhelmed by the amount of e-mail they received from colleges each day featuring sports, special programs, electronic media centers, and stately granite buildings set on idyllic grassy knolls or downtown in bustling cities. Each brochure seems to say, "Choose me!" without giving any clues as to what would be required to actually attend that school. Is it any wonder that students feel overwhelmed? The goal has been set with no instructions on how to achieve it. Adding to the confusion, sharply rising college costs, enrollments, and student debt loads have touched off a debate about the role of higher education in the 21st century (Cohn, 2011) and whether it is "worth" the money.

Why go to college? Maybe a better question is, "What do you want to do for the rest of your life?" Education, career choices, and future earnings are all related to this decision. Do students today believe that they are preparing for college, or for life, or both? And what do we as their parents and teachers believe (Webb, 2013b)? In 1997, President Clinton referred to education as "the fault line between those who will prosper in the new economy and those who will not" (para. 1). His words are truer today than ever before.

The typical adult with a bachelor's degree (but no further education) will earn $1.42 million over a 40-year career, compared with $770,000 for a typical high school graduate. That $650,000 difference narrows somewhat, to $550,000, after factoring in the expenses of going to college and the 4 years of potential earnings that college graduates give up while they are in school (Cohn, 2011, 2013).

The College Board reported that in its most recent survey of college pricing, a "moderate" college budget for an in-state public college for the 2012–2013 academic year averaged $22,261. A moderate budget at a private college averaged $43,289 (Baum & Ma, 2013). The total price of a college education depends on how long a student is enrolled before completing a degree. Many students spend more than 4 years earning a bachelor's degree. Average time to degree is longer in public than in private non-profit institutions.

The statistics remain consistent as the years go by and the cost of college increases. Yet, in a 2011 survey conducted by the Pew Research Center, a majority of Americans (57%) said the higher education system in the United States fails to provide students with good value for the money they and their families spend. An even larger majority—75%—said college is too expensive for most Americans to afford (Cohn, 2011, 2013).

We all have heard about people who became highly successful without a college education, but they are in the minority. We know who they are because their unusual achievement stands out. People without an education and job-related skills have a more difficult time finding work because they are competing against those who have more training. Further, if parents do not have a college education, the chances are that their children also will not attend college, primarily because their children never receive practical advice on applying to and attending college (Plank & Jordan, 2001). The reverse is also true: If you went to college, your children are more than twice as likely to attend.

A new report from the National Student Clearinghouse Research Center dug deeper into graduation rates. It found that of the 1.9 million students enrolled for the first time in all degree-granting institutions in fall 2006, just more than half of them (54.1 percent) had graduated within 6 years. Another 16.1% were still enrolled in some sort of postsecondary program after 6 years, and 29.8% had dropped out altogether (Rampell, 2013). Fewer than six in 10 first-time college students finish 4-year degrees within 6 years (Rampell, 2013; Stengel, 2012).

Almost half of those who never enrolled or dropped out said college wasn't for them because they wanted to work and make money. Almost as many said they couldn't afford college. Yet, by age 33, according to the College Board, the typical college graduate has earned enough to compensate for the cost of attending a

3

4-year public college or university, and has made up for earnings passed up during the college years (Baum & Ma, 2013; Baum & Payea, 2004).

Some benefits of a college education are subtle, but real. The acquisition of knowledge is a very personal thing. People who go to college use the knowledge they acquire for the rest of their lives, and will continue to expand their knowledge and skills, express their thoughts more clearly in speech and in writing, grasp abstract concepts and theories, and increase their understanding of the world and community. College is likely to promote a love of learning in people as a result of developing new interests and passions.

Until people go away to college, their friends are acquired largely by circumstance from among their neighbors, the children they associate with in the first 12 grades of school, athletics teammates, religious education classmates, and other settings. Going away to college exposes an individual to a diverse group of people—some good, some not so good—and at a minimum, it provides more options from which to choose. The world is a rich place, full of places and experiences that can hardly be imagined by a person who never leaves his or her hometown. College exposes us to people from different national, ethnic, and religious groups, to different social and political ideas, to different income levels or ways of life, and even different ways of learning or absorbing information. A college education gives us courage to try new things, fosters our imagination to create new things, and gives us the freedom to think critically about everything we will ever see or hear in our lifetimes.

There are more than 4,000 colleges and universities (including all types) in the United States. Choosing from among them is a complex task. Some students, particularly those who are gifted, are concerned about college and begin planning for it as early as elementary school. That being said, there are still many high school students who approach college planning and selection with less thought than they give to purchasing a video game or a new item of clothing. Lacking a plan, they may make arbitrary decisions based on inadequate information culled from a website, friend, or relative, simply because they do not know how to define the personal criteria needed to make college and career decisions. Far too many teenagers are simply not aware of how colleges differ, or how they can match their individual needs, wants, and desires with what a particular college may have to offer.

For many high school students, college planning is a process that begins and ends arbitrarily and abruptly, without reflection. This process typically begins with participation in the Preliminary SAT®/National Merit Scholarship Qualifying Test (PSAT/NMSQT) during 11th grade, and ends with the receipt of acceptance or rejection letters from the schools to which the student applied. Between the two milestones—the PSAT and letters of acceptance—students must select colleges they want to attend, complete a number of standardized achievement tests, and submit their applications. For many, the information they gather during the 11th and 12th grade is deemed sufficient to make decisions. For gifted, highly creative, or high-achieving students, however, a much longer process is necessary.

Gifted students should be concerned about and begin planning for college as early as the seventh grade, although many think about it earlier. They tend to make short mental lists that swing from one extreme to another: from "brand name" colleges, such as Harvard, Yale, Princeton, and Stanford, to popular state or community institutions. Their angst increases with each school year, building toward an event such as taking the PSAT, SAT, or ACT test. For gifted students, college planning should be one step in a life development process that takes place between seventh and 12th grade. This process begins in early childhood with your child's self-awareness and ends with matching his or her needs with college offerings. Between those two points, you can expect your child to acquire many new skills and experiences, and grow with each activity. As your child grows in experience and self-awareness, he will be increasingly able to plan his future based on his talents, skills, interests, needs, values, and passions.

This guide is for parents and adolescents in the midst of the complex process of college and career planning. Parents, much of the book will speak to your concerns as you work with your child, but some sections are meant to be used by your child, and are therefore addressed to the student. Throughout the book you will find charts and checklists that will help you and your teen gradually come closer to selecting a list of appropriate colleges. While you and your child go through some of the exercises in the book, there are several things to keep in mind:

» There is no such thing as the perfect school. The college experience, like life, is a series of trade-offs. Most students should be able to identify several different types of schools appropriate for them. This does not mean that they would have identical experiences at each school, only that their experiences would be equally positive.

» The path from point A, knowing oneself, to point B, a satisfying college experience, does not necessarily follow a smooth progression. Adolescents develop intellectually, socially, and emotionally at inconsistent rates. They face the challenge of making a critical decision on college selection at a point in their lives when they have not finished "becoming themselves." Parents, teachers, and counselors should encourage students to think of college selection as the first step in what may ultimately be a multistep process. For example, the college environment suitable for a student's freshman and sophomore years may be unacceptable for the final 2 years, because the student—not the college—has changed. In such a case, transferring to another college is a realistic and positive option. This is an important point for the student who wants to attend a highly selective school, but does not have the qualifications to do so. A year at a less selective school may be followed by a transfer to the original school of choice if the student uses that year to prove that he or she is capable of working at a challenging level.

» The most selective colleges receive more than 10 applications for every freshman vacancy. Seven of the eight colleges and universities that make up the Ivy League have lowered their acceptance rates since 2012. In 2013, the acceptance rate for the "Ivies" ranged from a low of 5% to a high of 8%. According to *The New York Times*, "the trend to tiptoe toward increased selectivity seems to hold true whether the institution received more or fewer applications than last year" (Abrams, 2013b, para. 2). College selectivity is the "application-to-admit ratio," or the number of students admitted compared to the number of students who applied. The degree of selectivity at a school can change from year to year, depending on the number of students applying for admission and the number of slots the college has available. A large percentage of these applicants are highly qualified. Keep in mind that the admission rates at Ivy League and other highly selective institutions are exceptions to the norm; there are more than 2,000 four-year colleges and universities in the United States. If your adolescent aspires to a highly selective college, you can expect a highly competitive application review. Because your student's credentials will be examined so carefully and critically, knowing what he or she is up against before you begin can help make the college search more realistic.

Many college planning guides provide slick marketing tips for college applicants. But, unless the match between your child's needs and interests and the school's offering is truly a good one—and there is no way of knowing that without going through the kinds of activities proposed in this guide—students may be disappointed.

Students who can ask and begin to answer questions about themselves are on the road to developing self-awareness. When they can begin to ask and answer questions about colleges and relate those answers to themselves, they are prepared to begin the college selection process. Students *discover* themselves—that is, they identify personal values, aptitudes, and needs—and they learn how to conduct a college search through a multistep process. Ideally, this process should begin by seventh grade, with specific events occurring each subsequent year. However, the process can be shortened as it is in this book. Included at the end of this chapter is a timeline to help your child throughout the college planning process.

PARENTS PROVIDING SUPPORT AND ENCOURAGEMENT

College planning and ultimately the transition to college are life-changing events for most teens, but keep in mind that all teens will have different reactions to the process. Some start making lists of potential colleges before ninth grade, while others have not yet made plans for college at the start of 12th grade. One type of student may post rejection letters on a bedroom bulletin board, another may let the process affect her self-esteem, and a third student may take it in stride. Selecting a college is one of the first adult choices in life. There are no perfect solutions or clear-cut alternatives. It's an event that signals a transition to adulthood. Parents are often confused about how much guidance they can and should provide. You may teeter between withdrawal and taking over the process, not knowing how to strike a balance. You have an important role—becoming an informed consumer, and setting clear and realistic goals that reduce the pressure and keep things in perspective. You should support, encourage, and even empathize with your teenager, remembering your own experiences as a young adult. When you take time to learn about college planning and how it differs from your experience or that of someone you know, you can truly make a positive difference. As one student told her parents, "The best thing you did was to laugh at my jokes." She was talking about having perspective, or college planning without any angst.

Some things for parents to keep in mind include the following:

» Getting into a brand-name school does not improve one's life. Teaching and learning are often better in schools you've never heard of.

» Be a "guide on the side," gently encouraging your child, rather than an all-knowing "sage on the stage." Be ready and able to demonstrate an understanding of the pressures these students are experiencing. Provide support.

» Know the critical skills your child needs to make major decisions.

» Understand how he or she defines the important characteristics of his or her ideal college.

» Help your child find specific institutions that meet his or her individual needs.

» Set clear and realistic goals that reduce the pressure on your child and keep things in perspective.

» Think of yourself as a shepherd. Your job is to guide and protect. Some parents avoid interfering by withdrawing. Some parents are overbearing. Neither extreme is useful.

» Discuss college openly, gearing conversation toward what your son or daughter needs from a college and why—city or country environment, emphasis on Greek life, sports, student/faculty ratio, class size, special programs, etc.

» Listen to your child. Pay particular attention to what attracts him or her to certain schools.

» *Do not* type applications, correct essays, or call colleges for information for your child. When a student has questions, an admissions office would prefer to hear from the student.

» *Do* keep track of dates such as those for standardized tests, admissions deadlines, financial aid deadlines, and so forth. Adolescents experience considerable pressure during their last 2 years in high school. Often, they need someone else to keep track of some of the details, especially due dates.

» *Do* make photocopies of all applications because it's almost inevitable that a big typo will crawl onto the page and it will need to be redone. Proofread everything for errors, but do not make major changes. Again, be sure to make copies of completed applications.

» Discuss any limitations, such as cost, up front. Find out all you can about financial aid. If money is a problem, as it is for most people, discuss it rationally and explain that the family will need to take advantage of available scholarships, loans, or any other source of funds. But, don't restrict your child's choices based solely on cost, because some colleges provide financial aid to all of their students.

» The college planning process is part of a life development process in which there are no right answers. The process is different for every person because the goal is to make a match between your child's strengths and interests and college offerings. The college that is perfect for someone you know may be totally wrong for your child. Let your student make his or her final decisions and own the process.

» The college search is like an arranged marriage. Make the best match you can—love will come later.

COLLEGE PLANNING TIMELINE, GRADES 9–12

The search for the ideal college begins well before a student's senior year in high school. Many students start thinking about college as early as fourth and fifth grade. Parents should be open to their questions, because they are most receptive to advice when they are thinking about colleges and forming a picture of an "ideal" college. The following timeline may be helpful to guide students' questions and start them onto the path to planning for college. It provides tips on what students can do to make sure they are on schedule. Of course, teenagers have their own unique schedule. Give them accurate information and trust them to follow through on their own timetable.

Eighth Grade: Looking Toward Ninth Grade

The initial weeks of high school can be a rocky social and emotional adjustment. Students say the adjustment is easier if they join an extracurricular group and transition into high school with that group. Examples include sports, musical groups such as band, or theater groups.

During this year, you should discuss the transition to high school with your parents and guidance counselor. You need to develop a master plan that includes an academic plan listing courses required for high school graduation and courses you *want* to take during the next 4 years.

Ninth Grade

Enjoy! The next 4 years will shape you as a student and a person. Make friends, work hard, and use time wisely. Start building credentials by keeping a list of the activities you enjoy. Keep track of academic and extracurricular awards, partly because it's too difficult to recreate such a list when you need it for college applications.

By ninth grade, you should have looked at and evaluated all of the high school academic options available to you, such as a magnet school, Advanced Placement (AP) courses, or an International Baccalaureate (IB) program. Examine and evaluate options that may be available in your community. For example, do you have a passion for music? You might be able to usher musical performances. If you are interested in astronomy or black holes, involve the whole family and share your excitement.

By now you should have drafted a 4-year plan—a strategy that will help you decide the courses you need, and how you can use your in-school and after school hours most effectively. Build a flexible schedule that will accommodate time for studying, extracurricular activities, exercise, and relaxing.

Look at summer courses at the talent search programs where you can make new friends. Take an SAT or ACT test just to see how well you do.

Find out about the extracurricular activities you would like to become involved in. Look for activities that include community service or leadership opportunities. Share your talents with others by volunteering. Helping others is a great way to learn something about yourself. Pursue any hobbies or sports that interest you. Get involved.

Start a notebook of your activities and details about those activities. Four years is a long time to try to remember what you did and when you did it.

The more selective colleges will check to see whether or not your courses represent the most challenging program offered by your high school. If you want challenging courses in 11th and 12th grade, you need to take the prerequisites. Think about the following:

» What courses are required for high school graduation?
» How many years of each subject are required (or preferred) for college admission?
» What additional academic areas would you like to explore that are not offered by your high school (e.g., philosophy, archaeology)? Consider a summer program.
» What extracurricular activities do you want to fit into your schedule?
» What activities are you committed to that you want to continue?
» What activities do you want to eliminate?
» What portion of college costs will be your responsibility? Do you need to work during high school?

If your high school includes a career center or multimedia center, get to know the people who work there and the resources available. Some career centers or libraries offer computer-assisted college planning programs in addition to Internet programs, books, and websites. Not all sources are reliable, and you'll save time if you know those that are helpful.

Ask your guidance counselor if your school offers online courses or community college classes that can't be offered in a regular class because of insufficient staff or similar limits. If there is a community college in your hometown, it is probably listed online. Google "community college" or "college" and the name of your hometown or city. Ask if they offer online courses or onsite classes to high school students.

Read widely. Develop a plan that includes newspapers (e.g., your local paper, *The New York Times*, *USA Today*), magazines (news, business, sports, and special interest magazines), and books (biography, history, science fiction, adventure, novels, poetry, and drama). Exposure to different kinds of material will improve your vocabulary and language skills.

Plan your sophomore year carefully. Take courses that are appropriate for you. Colleges will look at the classes you chose, not just your grades, to get a sense if you are stretching. A strong college preparatory program that is well balanced will ultimately show off the very best "you."

Tenth Grade

Meet with your counselor and ask what you should do to prepare for the next 3 years.

Register for the PSAT/NMSQT) and take it for practice. Obtain a free Student Bulletin. Visit the College Board website to learn what the test is like, how students may prepare, and how scores are reported and used. Make sure you are practicing with the latest version of the test. The PSAT is offered in October. Be sure to sign up. Scores don't count this year—just take the PSAT for practice. See your guidance counselor for instructions on how to sign up. When you take the PSAT/NMSWT in your junior year, there are several ways to win scholarship money. So be sure you check the website and know what they are.

Through the PSAT, you may get mail from colleges and universities that are interested in students like you. Start a filing system to organize the information you receive. A couple of oversized shoe boxes may work for now, but later you will want something that is easier to use, such as file folders.

Become familiar with college reference books published by the College Board, Peterson's, Fiske, and other organizations. Visiting a local library or bookstore will help you get to know different types of reference materials and what each can do for you. When college admissions people visit your school, talk to them and listen carefully to what these representatives say.

Visit a nearby college and take a tour. Check to see whether your school has college CDs, videos, or a media library.

Take SAT Subject Tests at the end of 10th grade in any subjects in which you have done well but do not plan to continue studying in high school (e.g., biology, foreign language). Most students take the subject tests toward the end of their junior year or at the beginning of their senior year, but you should take tests in subjects such as world history, biology, chemistry, or physics as soon as possible after completing the corresponding courses, while the material is still fresh in your mind. For foreign language tests, you'll do better after at least 2 years of study.

Plan a meaningful summer activity. Consider an internship, volunteer work, travel, or spending time with someone who works in a career that interests you.

Get more involved in your favorite extracurricular activity. Look for leadership opportunities. Keep a record of accomplishments, performances, and awards, if appropriate. Colleges look for *depth* of involvement.

Continue reading a wide variety of materials. The more you read, the more your vocabulary will expand.

Look into careers. Investigate computer-assisted career guidance programs such as Career Occupational Preference System (COPS; http://www.edits.net/products/copsystem.html), Career Options (http://www.rileyguide.com/careers.html), SIGI3 (http://www.valparint.com), or DISCOVER (http://www.act.

org/discover). If your school doesn't have them, ask the nearest community college career center.

Find out whether or not your high school administers vocational aptitude tests, interest inventories, learning style inventories, or personality tests. Take all available assessment tests and make an appointment with your counselor or career center to discuss the results.

Become familiar with the *O*net Dictionary of Occupational Titles* (http://www.onetonline.org) and the *Occupational Outlook Handbook* (http://www.bls.gov/ooh; see Appendix B for more information on these and other resources). Pick one or two careers and read about them. Spend some time with someone who works in those fields.

Keep your grades up.

By the end of 10th grade, review your 4-year plan and high school transcript with your guidance counselor and parents. Plan for 11th grade by signing up for challenging academic courses, but leave time for rest, relaxation, family activities, your favorite extracurricular activities, and community service. You may wonder how you will have time for community service. If you block out the time in advance, it will happen.

One more thing. Many college majors and career paths offer highly intensive summer courses. Admission is highly selective. Math is a good example. If you are serious about your field, your 4-year plan should include these advanced programs. In math there is the highly competitive Ross program at Ohio State University (http://math.osu.edu/~ross). In science, there is Siemens (http://www.siemens-foundation.org). Telluride Association Summer Programs (TASP; http://www. tellurideassociation.org) and Davidson or Presidential Scholars in humanities are highly competitive programs. TASP is also free. There is also the need-based Jack Kent Cooke Foundation Young Scholars program (http://www.jkcf.org/scholarships/young-scholars-program). Students apply for the program in seventh grade, enter the program in eighth grade, and continue through high school. Successful participation in any of these programs will bolster applications for anything a participant wants to do.

If you participated in any type of enrichment, ask for letters of recommendation from your supervisor, camp director, formal or informal mentor, or others before you complete your summer and school year activities. Do not wait until later. You want these people to write about you when they remember you best. Ask that the letters be addressed to "To Whom It May Concern," and give the letters to your guidance counselor as soon as possible. Keep copies.

Eleventh Grade

Discuss college plans with your parents and counselor. Find out how college planning operates at your school and ask about resources available to you. If possible, your parents should make an appointment with your counselor. Family discussions with a student's counselor early in the year help clarify everyone's expectations.

Begin the college search process. If your school has a College Night, be sure to attend, and go to at least one area college fair. Speak with college representatives when they visit your school, even if you think you are not interested in the school they represent. Compare and contrast what they tell you, what you have read, and what you have seen for yourself.

Sign up for the October PSAT. This time the scores count! Your PSAT scores are used to determine your eligibility for the National Merit Scholarship and the National Merit Hispanic Scholarship. Obtain a Student Bulletin (free from the College Board) to learn what the test is like, how you may prepare, and how your scores are reported and used. (See http://www.collegeboard.com for more information.)

Make sure you are familiar with the most recent changes to the SAT or the ACT. Check with the colleges and universities that interest you and ask your target schools which test they prefer. Plan to take one or the other in the spring.

If your scores are not as high as you expected, consider taking a prep course. Remember, the cost of a course may not reflect its quality. Try to find one in which the instructor will analyze your answer sheet, provide you with specific information on your strengths and weaknesses, and offer tips and hints on how to raise your scores. There are websites that will do this too, such as Barnes & Noble's Sparknotes (http://www.sparknotes.com).

Take SAT Subject Tests in subjects you will complete at the end of this school year or in courses such as a foreign language, even if you plan to continue taking the courses in further depth.

Keep up a good level of academic achievement. This is the year that really counts. Balance work, play, and extracurricular activities. Colleges like to see an upward trend in your grade point average.

Request financial aid bulletins from all of your target schools and ask your guidance counselor how to access the Free Application for Federal Student Aid (FAFSA) online. If you intend to apply for student financial aid from the federal government, you will need to submit the FAFSA when you are in 12th grade. There is no charge for submitting this form. The FAFSA is also required by all state and many school student assistance programs. You will need your family's tax return from the last year. Go online to get the FAFSA and take your family through the process of completing one (http://www.fafsa.ed.gov).

If you want to play sports for a National Collegiate Athletic Association (NCAA) Division I or II team, register with the NCAA Clearinghouse (1-800-638-3731, or go to http://www.ncaa.org).

If you are taking AP courses and doing extremely well, consider taking AP tests. Questions about how students can get credit for AP tests is one of the most common questions asked at college information sessions. The answer is not a simple "yes" or "no." Choose carefully: Some colleges offer exemption, credit, or both for AP grades of 3, 4, or 5. Other schools do not reward your efforts with exemption or credit, but it's important to challenge yourself with advanced courses. If you take AP tests someplace other than your school—for example during a summer program—be sure that your grades are reported to your high school and sent to the college of your choice before the end of your junior year.

By the end of 11th grade, review your 4-year plan and high school transcript with your parents and guidance counselor. Are you satisfied with your progress? Are you accomplishing your goals? Make a list of eight to 10 colleges that you *might* attend and choose at least one thing you liked about each one.

Make a college planning portfolio that includes academic courses (including courses taken during the summer or after school), extracurricular activities, community service, achievements, and awards.

Make a College Planning Chart that lists testing dates for PSAT, SAT Subject, SAT/ACT, and/or AP tests.

Figure 1 is a checklist you can use to make sure you are on target.

Twelfth Grade

Keep your cool! Work hard, refine your writing skills. Choose courses that show the best you can be.

Review your list of colleges. You should have a file on each college you are considering. Can you narrow your list at this point?

Review admissions criteria for the schools that interest you. Send for applications. Go to each college website and fill out "request for information" forms so the colleges will know you are interested.

Many colleges use data from CSS/Financial Aid PROFILE® to provide nonfederal financial aid. Begin applying online at http://student.collegeboard.org/css-financial-aid-profile.

Begin the scholarship search. Check out http://www.fastweb.com and http://www.finaid.org. Complete and mail the FAFSA or submit it electronically. Pay attention to deadlines. There are federal and state deadlines, and your colleges may also have deadlines (http://studentaid.ed.gov/fafsa). Financial aid applications

---

College Planning Portfolio

Who Am I?

____ Consider a summer activity such as:

- ☐ a summer internship;
- ☐ travel;
- ☐ courses offered by talent search programs on a campus (i.e., the opportunity to acquire college credits and try out a college lifestyle); or
- ☐ a college planning seminar (offered by many colleges for a week or more to help you get a headstart on applications and other elements). More about these programs later.

Where Am I Going?

____ Create a chart that lists:

- ☐ application deadlines (including early action and early decision dates);
- ☐ financial aid deadlines (they are often different at different colleges);
- ☐ tests required by colleges that interest you;
- ☐ costs including student fees and the other extras;
- ☐ number and type of recommendations required; and
- ☐ interview deadlines and locations.

What Do I Like?

____ Develop a list of 8–10 colleges. Work up a comparison chart. Include factors that are important to you, and keep in mind the following factors:

- ☐ size (campus, number of students);
- ☐ geographic location (urban, rural, North, South, etc.);
- ☐ course offerings (Do they teach what you like?);
- ☐ cost (tuition, room and board, books, travel to and from home, etc.);
- ☐ available scholarships or tuition assistance programs;
- ☐ extracurricular activities (newspaper, sports, etc.);
- ☐ selectivity (degree of difficulty); and

Figure 1. Junior year checklist.

☐   faculty-student relationships including seminars.
☐   Can undergraduate students participate in research?
☐   Who teaches freshmen classes: professors or teaching assistants?

Requirements for Specific Majors
____   Are you interested in any of the following and are any of them "deal breakers"?
☐   student life including Greek life;
☐   special programs (e.g., study abroad);
☐   academic advising and career counseling procedures; and
☐   student access to required readings, laboratory space, and computer time.

Some Additional Points To Consider Include:
☐   E-mail colleges to request information and application forms for 6–10 colleges. If schools prefer that you use online applications, download them. Keep all information so you can avoid typing the same info repeatedly. Copy-paste is easier than retyping.
☐   Make appointments for personal interviews at colleges you plan to visit in the fall or winter.
☐   Recheck application deadlines. Start filling out application forms early in the fall. Learn how to complete an error-free application. Make extra copies of each application form. Use the copies for practice before completing the originals.
☐   Unless instructions say otherwise, type everything. If you can't type, consider using a computerized application. Have someone proofread every word on your application forms. Correct all errors.
☐   Make and keep copies of everything.
☐   Think about three teachers you might ask to write a recommendation for you. (You might wind up with 1 or 2.) Talk to each one about your favorite activities and academic subject and remind them if you won an award.

Figure 1. Continued.

☐ Your counselor may be asked for a letter of recommend-ation. List all of your activities and leadership positions. List your academic accomplishments. Don't expect that your counselor will remember your accomplishments if he or she is responsible for 500+ students.

Figure 1. Continued.

such as the FAFSA should be submitted as soon as possible after January 1, but no sooner, because the tax form you will need is not available until January 1.

Applying for early admission, early decision, or any other atypical admission is not to be taken lightly. It's a calculated risk. Find out the number of students who are admitted early and then make a decision. You have declared yourself as being very interested to a school if you apply early. If you aren't, wait for the regular pool of student applicants.

Identify at least two teachers and two other people who know you well and could write solid recommendations for you. If you are applying for early admission or early decision, line up rec-ommendations as soon as possible. Make appointments to see them to review your accomplishments and goals. Follow up. It is *your* responsibility to make sure that letters of recommendation arrive before the colleges' deadlines.

Sign up to retake the SAT or ACT if you think you can raise your scores. Make sure that your SAT or ACT scores are sent to your guidance counselor and the schools to which you are apply-ing. Review your scores with your guidance counselor and ask for an interpretation that relates to the schools you are considering.

Check out both the Common Application AND the Universal Common Application to see which colleges accept it. If all of the colleges that interest you are included on either application, you can complete one application and use it for all schools. Colleges and universities that accept the Common Application are listed at https://www.commonapp.org. Schools that accept the Universal

College Application are listed on the website http://www.collegedata.com/cs/content/universal_college_application_colleges.jhtml.

Find out when your high school registrar or guidance counselor sends your applications, transcripts, letters of recommendation, and supporting materials to the colleges. Early in December is typical, but some high schools set earlier deadlines. Early decision deadlines are usually in November. If your school does not send application forms and supporting material to the colleges for you, then *you* must be sure to send everything *on time*. Pay attention to deadlines.

Photocopy *everything* before sending the application packages to colleges, because applications can be lost in the mail or college servers can break down, losing all data. If you use the Common Application, be especially careful, because the technology that the Common Application depends on has been unreliable.

Review your high school transcript carefully. If some courses listed are not easy to identify, be sure to add a description of those courses. An example is an honors course that doesn't say "honors" in the course name. Also, be sure your school profile or transcript supplement is included.

Maintain or continue to improve your academic standing. Most colleges look unfavorably upon an applicant whose grades are falling. Schools will revoke admission for students whose grades have slipped. If one of your grades is falling, you may want to write a letter of explanation. And if you experienced a traumatic event but your grades didn't fall, tell the colleges (for example, a divorce in your family or a long illness or hospitalization that affected your grades). Use either the personal statement or essay question in the application to talk about how you managed. If neither are available, talk about the event and your reaction in a personal interview. Focus on how you felt—resilient, hopeful, good at solving problems, determined?

Visit the colleges you are seriously considering.

Update your college planning portfolio. Be sure to add recent achievements and new events that have occurred.

Practice for interviews. Ask someone to roleplay with you. Introduce yourself, tell the interviewer where you are from, and briefly tell something about you. Enunciate your name clearly. Some colleges place a lot of emphasis on interviews and some don't care. Anything that you can find out beforehand will ultimately be helpful.

If you haven't received any financial aid packages by April, call the colleges to make sure the necessary information arrived. Send the acceptance notice and a deposit to the college you have chosen. Shop for school supplies!

2 PLANNING FOR GIFTED STUDENTS
What Makes Them Different?

Isabel is able to read maps quickly, can plan routes, and is often nominated as the trip planner when her family and friends travel. In preparation for a college interview 300 miles away, she analyzed six different routes to find the most direct and scenic route. When the family reached their destination, Isabel was greeted by the interviewer, who casually asked, "How was your trip?" Isabel spent the half-hour interview explaining the six alternative routes and the reasons for her choice, missing an opportunity to ask for information that was not mentioned in the catalog and other material, as well as an opportunity to explain how and why she would be a good match for that college. If Isabel had practiced the college interview and understood its purpose, she might have been able to make the most of her interview opportunity.

In high school, Alex was fascinated by the relationship between the ideas of Einstein, Picasso, and James Joyce. He developed a paper, entitled "The Climate of Opinion in the Early 20th Century," relating Einstein's theory of relativity, Picasso's cubist work, and Joyce's *A Portrait of the Artist as a Young Man*. Alex's thesis was that a fragmentation of reality had occurred simultaneously in mathematics, art, and literature. Alex's social studies teacher noted that the paper was late and reduced his grade from A to B. The teacher also noted Alex's problem with deadlines in the college recommendations he prepared. Other teachers noted that Alex sometimes did not complete assignments at all. Because all of the work he completed was superb, his grades were usually B's and C's—averages of the As for what had been completed on time, the Bs for late work, and the Fs for assignments that were never turned in. Alex had a problem. He needed a college like St. John's College (whose two campuses are located in Annapolis, MD, and Santa Fe, NM) that would nurture his talents and passion for abstract conceptualization. But, how was he going to find such a school, and how was he going to get in?

Jack wrote award-winning poetry and created sensitive lyrics for musical productions. When his class graduated from high school, he wrote a commemorative limerick. The title, "O Pioneers!", paraphrased Willa Cather. Jack's English teacher constantly criticized Jack's elaborate creative compositions, focusing primarily on the structure of the language used, punctuation, and rules of grammar. Jack received Cs and Ds because he did not follow the teacher's specific grammatical model. He frequently was unable to produce what was expected; therefore, his grade point average was not spectacular. Jack was extremely gifted and needed to attend a school where his talents would be appreciated and developed, such as Grinnell College in Iowa or Middlebury College in Vermont, both small liberal arts schools. However, with his grade point average, he had to communicate clear goals and actively persuade a college that he was capable of college-level work.

Nadia was the exception, even among students who are highly gifted. She was not an academic superstar. In fact, she camouflaged her talents because she wanted to appear similar to other students in her gifted class. She believed that no one understood her interests. Early college entrance offset some of Nadia's loneliness. She needed to go to college at age 13 (Solow & Rhodes, 2012). Early Entrance College Programs provide a peer group and academic challenge but do not solve all the problems. Some teens need to be with their families. Not all enrollees adjust. Nonetheless, early entrance programs have grown in popularity, primarily because they are closer to meeting the needs of profoundly gifted children than acceleration within a public or private school, or homeschooling. You will find a list of Early Entrance College Programs in Appendix A.

Gifted students are a diverse group. The above vignettes describe students who are gifted and quite different from one another, although they appear to have certain intellectual and social/emotional traits in common.

They are not necessarily recognized or identified as gifted, but they have some of the characteristics of gifted students that affect their college planning. Two of these traits are multipotentiality (multiple talents) and intense sensitivity (Webb, 2013a) to competing expectations as well as emotions and sensory stimuli. Other special populations of gifted students we'll discuss include students who are learning disabled, homeschooled students, and underachieving gifted students.

MULTIPOTENTIAL GIFTED STUDENTS

Keesha is a multipotential multitalented gifted student. As a high school junior, she had boundless enthusiasm for everything and an endless supply of energy. Her interests included psychology, creative writing, language, physics, chemistry, jewelry making, dancing, swimming, being outdoors, science fiction, and "people." The lead cross country runner in her grade, she was also in the top 10% of her grade and had already taken AP English. Keesha had a strong desire to be of service to humanity, and she wanted to master 12 languages before she turned 40.

If the above vignette sounds like your gifted student, you may be anxiously looking forward to the day she will get a driver's license, and be able to drive to all of her activities alone. Gifted students are highly capable, and many participate in a variety of activities. Often, their calendars present an intimidating display of appointment dates and times. Many multitalented students have heard the saying "You can be anything you want" over and over again. But that is precisely the problem: They seem to suffer from a wealth of abilities. Some of these youngsters excel in every academic subject and activity. Keesha wonders how she will be able to make college and career plans when, on the surface, she likes everything and is good at everything. Students like her experience vocational selection as an existential dilemma. They are as concerned about the road not taken as they are with finding the right path. For Keesha, choosing to be a linguist means giving up a career as a physicist. Many underchallenged secondary students fill up their lives with many activities, either to avoid boredom or because they think they need to appear to be well-rounded for future college applications. If this attitude is carried over into the college setting, the attempt to participate in everything may create a destructive academic and emotional environment. It is much better to choose a few activities and focus on them, eventually assuming a leadership role.

Vocational exploration and aptitude tests, intended to provide guidance by showing students their areas of strength and matching those strengths to careers, are of little use to students like Keesha, because these tests showed evenly high aptitudes, abilities, and interests in every area.

SENSITIVITY TO EXPECTATIONS

Marcus is the middle child of three. His parents expected that all of their children would excel in school, and indeed his older and younger sisters were always on the honor roll and succeeded in everything they did. In school, Marcus was more interested in making friends than in earning grades, and when his grades began to drop in eighth grade, his parents sent him to a private school that instilled in him a solid respect for achievement. Marcus attended an Ivy League college, followed by law school. He passed the bar with flying colors and opened a law office. But something wasn't right. Marcus was unhappy. One day he closed his practice and went to Hollywood to become an actor. Marcus was exceptionally sensitive to expectations. His parents never had to say anything because he knew that high achievement and a profession were expected. But, he had a passion for acting, one that had never been fulfilled. Fortunately, he was young enough to change careers and realized that law was never going to provide the inner satisfaction he needed.

Sensitivity and receptivity are great assets, and they permit a student to be receptive to imaginative, creative ideas. Like multipotentiality, however, these characteristics can be a mixed blessing when students plan for college and a career. Parents, relatives, friends, siblings, teachers, and coaches—all with the best of intentions—are eager to add their own expectations and observations to the bright student's intentions and goals. The dilemma is complicated by the numerous options within the reach of a highly talented student.

Heightened sensitivity is often accompanied by heightened vulnerability to criticism, suggestions, and emotional appeals from others. Often, others' expectations for talented young people compete with the pull of their own dreams and plans. Some youngsters do not even think about what they want. They become so conflicted by all of the advice they receive that they postpone going to college or attend college and change their major several times, prolonging their graduation.

GIFTED STUDENTS WITH DISABILITIES

Over the past decade, clinicians and practitioners have devoted extraordinary time and energy to providing parents and teachers with clues for identifying children with learning and other disabilities. Parents, however, often sense that their child is somehow different long before they receive confirmation from a consulting psychologist or the school. According to Wrightslaw (2013):

> Twice-exceptional children are gifted children of above average abilities who have special educational needs - AD/HD, learning disabilities, Asperger Syndrome, etc. Because their giftedness can mask their special needs and their special needs can hide their giftedness, they are often labeled as "lazy" and "unmotivated." (para. 2)

Disabilities can affect gifted students in many areas, whether it is difficulty paying attention or staying on task, or specific identified learning disabilities such as dyslexia. At home or at school, your child may be oblivious to time, may appear to be lazy, forgetful, or unprepared, or may honestly believe that a project or chore has been completed when it has hardly begun. She may have trouble concentrating on completing rote assignments or classroom lectures, but can spend hours engaged in research on a topic of her interest. He may have difficulties reading and comprehending material and need assistive technology, such as books on tape, to get him through long reading assignments.

But, what happens if your child has disabilities and is gifted? Gifted students with disabilities (often known as twice-exceptional) have much in common with other gifted students. They typically have an excellent long-term memory, an extensive vocabulary, and grasp abstract concepts, thriving on complexity. They are highly creative, imaginative, perceptive, and insightful, and they are keen observers. They also have much in common with other students who have learning disabilities, such as a poor short-term memory and poor organizational skills. Their handwriting is frequently illegible, they struggle with easy, sequential material, and rote memorization is almost impossible. They may be unable to learn unless they are interested in the topic. These students perform poorly on timed tests. Yet, only a small percentage of gifted students with learning disabilities are identified, in part because they use their giftedness in ways that compensate for their limitations. Thus, the giftedness masks the learning disability, and the disability masks the giftedness, so that neither is visible in the classroom.

Giftedness may combine with almost any area of disability. Each combination is unique, but many twice-exceptional people are highly accomplished. For example, take Matt Savage, a young man with autism who is an internationally known jazz pianist. Matt was awarded the American Society of Composers, Authors and Publishers (ASCAP) Young Jazz Composer award in 2005 (see http://www.savagerecords.com). Children with Williams Syndrome (see http://www.williams-syndrome.org), a rare genetic condition that causes medical and developmental problems, may be superbly musical, and despite their difficulties, many are professional musicians. The ACM Lifting Lives Music Camp is a week-long residential camp designed for people with Williams syndrome who are at least 16 years old (http://kc.vanderbilt.edu/). Children with Asperger's syndrome seem to soak up knowledge and develop expertise in areas of interest; however, they have severe problems with social skills. Children with dyslexia often have a high level of spatial intelligence (West, 1997). Children with Attention Deficit/Hyperactivity Disorder (ADHD) have many talents and strengths. They may be able to do double-digit subtraction in their heads, but can't concentrate long enough to learn things that most children find simple. Children with executive functioning disorders cannot get organized in the traditional sense of the word. For gifted children with disabilities, the more difficult and complex tasks may be the easiest; however, simple tasks may be beyond their capabilities. Some are placed in gifted programs where their low grades are chalked up to laziness or bad attitude. Others languish in special education classes where they are literally bored to tears by drill-and-kill math exercises and too-simple reading primers. Then, there are those students whose gifts and disabilities are so evenly balanced that they are presumed to be average and left to fend for themselves in mainstream classes (Baum, 1990).

The following case study and discussion of the college and career planning process makes clear how infinitely more complex that process may be when the gifted adolescent has significant learning disabilities.

When he was an infant, a major university hospital identified Anthony's brain abnormalities as resulting from birth trauma. His parents were told they were lucky his troubles were identified so early in his life. During his early childhood, different medical professionals diagnosed Anthony's problems as a variety of disorders, including mental retardation, brain damage, dyslexia, minimal brain dysfunction, and learning disabilities. His IQ scores varied from below average to above average, depending on which person evaluated him. Recommendations for Anthony's schooling ranged from placement in a therapeutic day nursery, to a special education facility, to a mainstream environment. His parents were told many different, conflicting things, including that he either needed a self-contained class, a resource class, or no special arrangements at all.

One expert said Anthony was perfectly normal, suffering only from overanxious parents. Others blamed his problems on assorted psychological experiences, none related to birth trauma or learning disability. Anthony progressed through the expected developmental stages, but always at his own unique pace. He walked with difficulty, and at age 3, he could barely talk. In nursery school he made progress in gross motor skills and reading readiness. His fine motor skills were very poor, and his social skills were nonexistent.

At age 5, Anthony began to read, developed a rich vocabulary, made insightful, though garbled, comments, and accelerated rapidly in reading skills. Preschool teachers missed the signs of his giftedness, focusing instead on toilet habits and his inability to write his name legibly. A private school specializing in children with learning disabilities proved inappropriate. At home he read every book given to him, but the school proudly reported that he had mastered "three new letters this quarter." The school admitted it was impeding his academic progress.

When he was ready for elementary school, Anthony asked to enter public school. He knew he had difficulties and worked harder than his peers to achieve modest results. Despite hours of assistance, he could not remember recently learned facts and had difficulty following simple directions. Arithmetic proved almost insurmountable. He felt academically superior in self-contained classrooms but could not cope with impersonal regular classes. Socialization remained a problem.

By high school, his reading level was excellent, and his understanding of content was accurate and compassionate. He developed a keen interest in computers. His speech was still difficult to understand, his memory was spotty, and he could not learn arithmetic or write a coherent sentence. The school's protocol for planning an academic program allowed maximum mainstreaming and capitalized on Anthony's strengths and wishes. His preferences led to family negotiations about subjects he needed or were important, or where he would do well, might fail, or need help. He took courses no special education student had taken (e.g., 3 years of foreign language and 2 years of computer science). He refused, over the school's objection, to take traditional special education courses. Despite this approach, some teachers resisted his presence, and others placed meaningless burdens on him.

By his senior year, it was clear that Anthony had an exceptional mind for specific areas of study. His reading and vocabulary abilities were significantly above grade level, he had a knack for computer science, and he developed a strong interest in and understanding of politics. He still could not do arithmetic, spell, or write legibly, but he finished high school with a fine record and was elected to the National Honor Society. He certainly had learning disabilities, but clearly demonstrated traits and characteristics associated with giftedness.

After an extensive search for colleges with support programs, one was identified that met all the criteria that had been set. He took courses offered to the entire student body, but received tutorial support in all subject areas. By his junior year, he had made the Dean's List and was elected into a national scholastic honor society. Anthony graduated and went on to earn a master's degree in experimental psychology, challenged again by a professor more focused on legibility than content. Now, Anthony holds a professional computer technology position with the federal government, is married, has a son, and owns his own home.

Special Concerns

The decision to send a child with learning disabilities to college (regardless of his or her giftedness) is not one to be taken lightly by a student or his or her parents.

> The parenting dynamic often has to change a great deal. Many parents of 2E kids find themselves in a pattern of rescuing the kids from painful situations. As the kids move towards adulthood, not only is it less appropriate for parents to be in that role, the kids often don't want the parents to be there either. They may not express themselves clearly on that topic; sometimes what they do appears to be overconfidence, rejection, or self-sabotage. (Yermish, 2010)

For students with deficits in relevant skills—social, study, and organizational skills—it is a major decision. Support systems meticulously worked out in high school cannot follow the student to college. Parent advocacy must be replaced by self-advocacy. Academic learning must be pursued while a medley of independent living skills is developed, friends are sought, and separation from home and family is realized. The student with learning disabilities of any kind who is thinking of attending college must be made aware of all of these difficulties and understand that the choice to attend or not to attend is his or her own decision to make. Further, colleges are most welcoming to students who have "overcome" their disabilities, those who are accomplished in spite of them. That does not mean that disabilities have somehow magically disappeared, but rather, that the student can accomplish any goal he or she sets.

Once your gifted and learning disabled child realizes that he or she is capable of attending a college, the personal (Who am I?) and college (Who are they and what will they expect of me?) evaluations should begin. Discussions also should begin with guidance counselors and college advisers. Just like with any other college-bound student, there are college fairs to attend, guides and directories to review, visits to be made, and applications to be completed.

Like all gifted students, children with disabilities need to understand their own abilities and limitations, and guide their own transition planning by looking at various postsecondary options. For a student with learning disabilities, the basic college planning steps and schedules are similar in many ways to those for a more typical student. Your child needs to become familiar with how he or she learns best. Many successful students with learning disabilities acquire compensatory learning strategies to help them use the knowledge they have accumulated, to plan, complete, and evaluate projects, and to take an active role in shaping their environments. Your child needs to learn how to apply learning strategies flexibly, and how to modify or create strategies fluently to fit new learning situations. For example, compensatory strategies may include:

» allowing more time to complete tests, papers, and other projects;
» listening to audio tapes of textbooks while reading; and
» making up words to remind your child to use his or her prior knowledge.

You and your child with a learning disability must expand upon the basics of college planning and focus on specific, unique issues. For example, you must learn to distinguish between schools that merely accept students with learning disabilities as a condition of continuing federal support from those that actively encourage the enrollment of these students by providing specialized programs for them. You must also investigate the school's support to determine whether it is unstructured (provided as needed) or structured (records on the student are maintained and progress is monitored).

As the list of college criteria is assembled, you and your child must be honest about your perceptions of his or her needs. Basic questions, such as the school's distance from home and available transportation for home visits, single-sex education or coeducation, the size of the student body, and academic standing, must be expanded to include issues such as the following:

» Is there evidence of an organized program to aid students with learning disabilities?
» Is there evidence of a full-time or part-time staff in the program, as well as someone to monitor activities?
» Is there evidence of special considerations for learning disabled students, such as allowing tape recorders in the classroom, untimed tests, writing laboratories, tutors in every subject area, and allowance of extended time for graduation?
» Is there evidence of successful career placements of students in their chosen fields following graduation?

After your child determines his or her list of schools, the schools must then be contacted, interviews arranged, and family visits planned. Campus tours and the opportunity to sit in on classes must be given particular attention, because it is extremely important for your child to personally judge the level of difficulty of the instruction, observe the interaction of other students, and gain a sense of the relationship between the students and the faculty.

The admissions interview may not answer all of the questions regarding programs designed for gifted students with learning disabilities. If this is so, you and your child must seek out and meet with a member of the learning disabilities program staff. A list of questions based on family concerns and perhaps stimulated by a review of the college directories and guides or discussions with high school guidance personnel should be prepared prior to the visit. Questions might include the following:

» What type of support is available for students with disabilities?
» Does a professional staff monitor the program?
» Has the program been evaluated, and if so, by whom?
» Are there any concerns for the program's future?
» Who counsels students during registration, orientation, and course selection?
» For which courses is tutoring available?
» What kind of tutoring is available, and who does it—peers or staff?
» Is tutoring automatically provided, or must the student request assistance?
» How well do faculty members accept students with learning disabilities?
» May students take a lighter load each semester instead of the traditional 12–15 hours?
» Are courses in study skills or writing skills offered?
» Have counselors who work with these students received special training?
» How do students on campus spend their free time? Are there programs that will interest and accommodate them?
» May students take more time to graduate?

» Who can parents contact if they have concerns during the academic year?

» Is assistive technology available or permitted in the classroom? (Word processors with text-to-speech software, outlining, word prediction, and speech recognition capabilities offer assistive capabilities depending on a person's specific disabilities.)

The adolescent's progress toward adulthood is constantly stymied by dilemma. The dilemma faced by students, most particularly gifted students with disabilities, stems from their desire to demonstrate independence from parents, counselors, teachers, and tutors, and the equally strong desire to maintain the respect and support of those same parents, counselors, teachers, and tutors. Students frequently wish to make the decisions that will frame their future, even while sensing that they may not be realistic or ultimately doable.

College and career planning for gifted students with disabilities is practical, but it requires extraordinary participation, cooperation, and patience.

The best way to prepare children is by preparing them for the future, letting them see what they are capable of, and arming them with skills, work habits, and inner confidence that no one can ever take away. (Webb, 2013a)

Legal Issues

The 2004 update of the Individuals with Disabilities Education Act (IDEA; 1990) requires that the Individualized Education Program (IEP) team consider postschool goals when the student is about to enter high school at about age 14. Beginning at age 16 (or younger, if appropriate) a statement of transition services needed by the student must be included in the IEP. Once students with disabilities graduate from high school, they are no longer eligible for services provided by the school system, including an IEP.

The Office for Civil Rights in the U.S. Department of Education says that if schools "condition" participation in accelerated classes or programs by qualified students with disabilities by requiring these students to forfeit their necessary special education or related aids and services, it amounts to a denial of FAPE under Part B of the IDEA and Section 504 (Wrightslaw, n.d., para. 9).

The Americans with Disabilities Act (ADA; 1990) bars discrimination against students with disabilities during the college admissions process. Once admitted, students may request reasonable accommodations to allow them to participate in courses, exams, and other activities. Most colleges and universities have a disability support services office to help provide accommodations.

The following suggestions may help those who guide gifted students with learning disabilities:

» Students must understand their strengths and learning needs not only to be successful in coursework, but also to identify and request the accommodations they will require.

» Colleges require documentation of a disability (i.e., results of tests indicating the presence of a disability) in order to provide support services; having an IEP or Section 504 plan in high school is not enough documentation to obtain services from colleges.

» Students should be informed that there are several forms of the SAT, ACT, and many other standardized tests. Students may request to take an untimed version of the SAT or the ACT, but arrangements must be made well in advance. For more information, check out the Services for Students with Disabilities website at http://student.collegeboard.org/services-for-students-with-disabilities.

» Students who might have difficulty completing a typed college application should investigate a computerized method of completing a college application.

HOMESCHOOLED STUDENTS

Matt was a very bright child with a quick mind who mastered schoolwork easily. By the time he reached second grade, it was obvious to his parents that he was getting bored and the public school was no longer a match for Matt's abilities. At first, his parents were reluctant to homeschool Matt and his older brother, because neither parent had attended college. However, his parents did opt to homeschool the brothers, and when needed, the family readily sought outside help, especially in curricular areas where the parents had little expertise.

The boys thrived in this environment and participated in Little League sports for many years. Matt's basketball team was made up of homeschooled students. Because the brothers were homeschooled and moved through the curricula at their own pace, the family had great flexibility and had time for many types of activities. At age 12, Matt became the youngest student ever to enroll in the local junior college. Completion of a series of junior college classes enabled Matt to complete 18 hours of college courses before graduating from high school. Matt's mother kept a highly detailed transcript of his courses and activities. His first-choice school, Baylor University, a large private university, accepted Matt's application for enrollment.

Matt says that homeschooling gave him an independence that served him well in college. His advice to current high school students who are homeschooled? "Do not let the pace of your public school peers dictate to you the pace of your dreams. Don't wait until you're a college sophomore before you start identifying your gifts and dreams and setting goals toward achieving those dreams." Matt graduated from Baylor after 4 successful years, excelling academically, socially, and as a member of the university's Student Government.

Are you a homeschooling parent? If so, your children are part of the more than 1 million students in the U.S. who are homeschooled. If your adolescent is in high school, you may have wondered about the transition into college. If college admission is so competitive, how are you going to help your homeschooled teen stand out?

The homeschool scene has changed in remarkable ways. For example, Harvard's website provides the following details on their offerings for homeschooled students (https://college. harvard.edu). As a homeschooled student, you can enroll in courses to earn credit toward high school graduation, prepare for college, or study a subject unavailable at your school. No application is required. Harvard has more than 650 courses in 60 subjects, including expository writing, foreign languages, math, and biological sciences. They offer 200 distance education courses, some of which are Harvard classes. Some homeschooled students choose to pursue the Associate in Arts degree as an alternative to high school. You may then apply to traditional undergraduate degree programs as a transfer student or as a freshman with some college experience. You may also earn an undergraduate degree in the Extension School's Bachelor of Liberal Arts program.

Keep a Journal

Parents who are homeschooling secondary students will find that keeping a journal is key to sanity, because it's almost impossible to recreate 4 to 6 years of school for a college application. The journal can be anything you want it to be, but some items are necessary, such as lists of courses taken and texts used, and examples of your child's work, such as essays, reading logs, sheets of math problems, and photographs of him or her doing lab work. If your teen needs advanced subjects in one or more academic areas where you don't have expertise, you have probably looked for someone with advanced skills and the interest to serve as a mentor. If possible, it would be helpful if that person also kept a journal, or some type of record that would document your child's path through high school.

Extracurricular or Outside Activities

If your child wishes to attend a competitive college or apply for scholarships, he or she should participate in extracurricular activities to demonstrate that there is more to life than academics. Homeschoolers have a distinct advantage in this area. They may not have the resources of a traditional school, but they have the time to be involved in activities other than those offered at a traditional high school. For example, one homeschooled student who was interested in political science interned for a state delegate and lobbied on Capitol Hill. Other students have started their own magazine instead of working on the school paper. Others have gone on overseas missions trips. College-bound homeschoolers should use the extra time they have gained from individualized learning to gain real-world experiences that are growth promoting and look good on college and scholarship applications. However, activities should not be undertaken solely because they will look good. There needs to be interest and a passion.

Taking Tests

Many homeschooled students are concerned about taking tests, because they haven't had much practice. The SAT is scheduled to undergo radical changes in 2016, and you should familiarize yourself with the scoring quirks that accompany any complex test. On the Barnes & Noble Sparknotes website you can find lots of materials to assist you in studying. For more information, visit http://www.sparknotes.com.

Statistics from the SAT and ACT college entrance exams (Ray, 2003; Rudner, 1999) indicated that homeschooled students do perform competitively compared to traditional students. In 1999, students who identified themselves as homeschooled scored an average of 1083 out of 1600 on the SAT, 67 points above the national average, and an average score of 22.7 on the ACT, compared with the national average of 21. Sixty-nine percent of homeschoolers go on to college, compared with 71% of public high schools graduates and 90% of private school graduates. How do they get in without transcripts? Parents put together portfolios with samples of their children's work and lists of their accomplishments. Transcripts are created at home, and standardized test scores are included in the portfolio. The College Board provides specific instructions on its website for homeschoolers taking AP tests.

One of the problems encountered by homeschooled students is the potential for fewer contacts with college admission representatives. College representatives typically visit high schools to provide information to students and look for student academic stars, musicians, athletes, and so forth. Students enrolled in high school can take advantage of the interaction with college staff by asking questions about the school, lifestyle, academic rating, and anything else that is important. Homeschooled students need to find other ways to interact with college staff from a wide range of postsecondary institutions. College fairs provide that opportunity. The National Association for College Admission Counseling (NACAC) website (http://www.nacacnet.org) offers a list of college fairs and their locations and dates.

Colleges now consider the use of portfolios, a transcript prepared by a parent, and SAT and ACT results as legitimate methods of assessing homeschooled students' preparation for college. More than two thirds of American colleges now accept parent-created transcripts, although some require homeschooled applicants to submit a GED or additional standardized test scores that provide admissions officers the necessary context for assessing students' abilities (NACAC, 2005). It's best if your adolescent asks the school he or she is interested in what it expects in terms of objective information (e.g., GPA, class rank, test scores). Some schools actively recruit homeschoolers, because they tend to be highly focused and goal oriented. Harvard University, Purdue University, and the University of Texas are all homeschooler-friendly and impart some good advice for anyone interested in attending the school.

UNDERACHIEVING STUDENTS

> Alicia (an identified gifted ninth-grade student) could not put her name on the paper. She was afraid that it would not be "right." She could not answer in class. She could not hand in written work.
>
> —Teacher of gifted students

Alicia was under the care of a clinical psychologist. Her psychologist, parents, teachers, and counselor knew that she was capable of functioning at an extremely high intellectual level. They persuaded her to enroll in a seminar designed for gifted students, hoping that she would eventually respond to the special teaching strategies and peer support. Everyone encouraged Alicia, despite occasional feelings of doubt. One day in class, Alicia tentatively raised her hand. By the end of the semester, Alicia was responding to the intellectual stimulation provided by her teacher and classmates. She was able to turn in assignments and participate in class discussions. When Alicia applied to college 3 years later, her application was accepted.

> In seventh grade, Jason scored 1500 out of 1600 on the SAT. His grades, however, were mediocre. The only thing he seemed to care about was computers and computer games. It was obvious that he didn't have to put forth any effort to earn high grades; however, he didn't seem to care and frequently didn't hand in assignments. He seemed to need a sense of purpose.
>
> —Parent of a gifted student

When Jason applied to college, his transcript reflected a series of ups and downs—grades that ranged from A to F. His grade point average was less than remarkable, reflecting his tendency either to turn in work that teachers considered brilliant, or not turn in his assignments at all. His standardized test scores reflected high ability and high aptitude in all areas. His test scores included grades of 4 and 5 on AP Examinations, and he had entered a national mathematics competition and excelled.

Jason's parents and teachers thought of him as brilliant, but unmotivated. His guidance counselor described him as "an unharnessed dynamo." When he applied to college, his application was rejected everywhere. His guidance counselor called several colleges and discovered that Jason was identified as a risky applicant, in part because he had high scores on standardized tests and a low grade point average (GPA). The counselor, having spent several years persuading Jason to remain in high school, decided to argue on his behalf. The counselor was successful, and Jason was admitted to a highly selective college. Although Jason's college grades were less than admirable and he continued to feel frustrated with educational structure, he earned a college degree. The guidance counselor's support provided Jason with an opportunity to take one step toward fulfilling his potential.

> It was difficult to convince Anna, age 15, to take AP courses. She felt she could not succeed academically and continue to help support her family.
>
> —Guidance Counselor

Anna's parents, who were culturally diverse, struggled to earn a living. When Anna was recommended for AP courses, her family objected. The expectations of high academic achievement and postsecondary education on the part of both the teachers and students were different from those of her family and neighbors. Her father expected that Anna would complete high school and work in the family grocery store. Her mother worried that Anna would lose her cultural identity if she enrolled in highly rigorous courses. Despite family protests, Anna took advantage of every academic opportunity. When she applied to college, her family argued that she should enroll in the local community college, in part because they knew they could not afford tuition, room, and board anywhere else. Her counselor argued that Anna could attend any college she wanted. Several highly selective colleges accepted Anna's application. Her counselor watched for possible scholarships and, whenever possible, argued the merits of Anna's case.

The above vignettes are examples of students who were labeled underachieving during high school. These gifted students are quite different from one another. They do, however, share two attributes: their potential and a counselor, teacher, or parent who recognized that potential and decided to encourage the student.

If your child exhibits many of these characteristics consistently and for more than one year, he or she may be underachieving in school:

» inattentiveness;
» disorganization;
» does homework carelessly or incompletely;
» "forgets" to turn in assignments even they are when completed;
» procrastinates until the night before;
» disruptive in some classes;
» argumentative;
» asks for more help than necessary;
» blames others;
» makes excuses;
» avoids competition;
» considers school boring; or
» interest in learning has declined in school, as well as at home.

The idea of an underachieving gifted student is seen by many to be an oxymoron. How can a student be gifted and not succeed in school? Research studies often raise more questions than they answer. These students do not live up to expectations, causing their parents and teachers frustration. But, whose expectations are they not living up to? Is potential measurable or, in the words of Charlie Brown, is potential the "world's heaviest burden"? Are we describing gifted students who are experiencing academic difficulty and feel uncomfortable, or are we describing parents, teachers, or counselors who expect more than a student is willing and able to produce?

Underachieving gifted students are often described in terms of significant inconsistencies in measured ability and grades earned in school. For example, Jason was identified as gifted at an early age through the use of the Wechsler Intelligence Scale for Children (WISC-IV). His standardized test scores reflected high ability and aptitude in all areas; however, he earned mediocre grades in many high school subjects.

Some students are silent underachievers—no one knows how capable they are because they haven't had opportunities to demonstrate their advanced reasoning. Students whose capabilities are a total mismatch with the curriculum may not be recognized as gifted (Baum, 1990; Delisle & Berger, 1990). We may not know the ability level of a particular student who camouflages giftedness under satisfactory performance, especially if the student's teachers, counselor, and parents have no evidence to indicate that the student is gifted. Many gifted students with disabilities fit into this group of underachievers—giftedness and the learning disability mask one another. Some of these students may have been recognized as having a disability, but no one recognized their potential. Or, they may have been recognized as gifted, but could not negotiate an expanded curriculum.

Specific personality traits, conditions, and behaviors such as impulsiveness, depression, low self-esteem, lack of motivation, inability to concentrate for long periods of time, inconsistent work habits, perfectionism, and fear of failure have also been identified and viewed as both an influence on and an effect of long-term underachievement (Siegle, 2013). Some of these characteristics and behaviors, however, have been observed in eminent adults. An analysis of autobiographies such as *Surely You're Joking, Mr. Feynman!* (Feynman, 1985) and *The Autobiography of Eleanor Roosevelt* (Roosevelt, 1958) indicates that eminent adults who have made significant contributions to society share some of these characteristics. Underachievement cannot be understood when approached solely from the perspective of student characteristics; rather, the problem is multidimensional.

Most experts believe that underachievement is related to a number of factors, some within the child, some within the environment, and some due to a mismatch of the two (Reis & McCoach, 2002). Most interventions have been met with limited success, and were designed for immediate results with a population of severely underachieving children (Supplee, 1990; Whitmore, 1980). These interventions consist of carefully crafted environments with a smaller teacher–student ratio and highly trained teachers.

Felice Kaufmann, a researcher and educator with extensive experience working with gifted students, believes that underachievement is a defensive behavior that protects against feelings of profound discouragement. Kaufmann has described underachieving gifted students as discouraged individuals who need encouragement, but tend to reject praise as artificial or inauthentic. Excessive praise may strengthen the underachiever's belief that she is acceptable only when she is doing something that is valued by others. In other words, "cheerleading" is unlikely to provide these students with the necessary ammunition to cope with their problems (F. Kaufmann, personal communication, August 1989). She found that underachieving gifted students have difficulty committing work to paper, tend to lack confidence, avoid responsibility, avoid competition, may be highly resistant to adult and peer influence, and may be highly perfectionistic, sensitive, and vulnerable. These students may respond to counseling, although counseling too has been met with limited success. Often, the counselor's goal is to help the student decide whether academic achievement is a desired aspiration (Reis & McCoach, 2002).

College planning for an underachieving gifted student is a bit of a conundrum, because it involves a match between student needs and school offerings. An underachiever is going to have a difficult time making that match. On the one hand, gifted students are motivated by and need topics and experiences that interest them. They respond positively to appropriate instructional strategies. Often, that leaves the student with four options: (1) a small private college with counseling available as part of the curriculum; (2) a 2-year community college where a student can learn to work at a more challenging level for a couple of years and then transfer to a 4-year school; (3) an additional year of secondary school at a private school before moving into a collegiate environment; or (4) an internship or volunteer position where the student can spend time providing a needed service and learn something about the world of work. Many students choose to do a postgraduate year at a private school to improve their chances for admission to a selective or highly selective college. A postgraduate year is beneficial for strengthening academic skills and may give students a chance to mature. It also helps if the student can write an essay about the year and explain what was learned. Some students enroll in community colleges to raise their GPA. Community colleges do not usually provide an appropriate peer group for gifted students or an appropriate level of instruction. Without counseling, the student may repeat the same patterns as in high school. Private high schools are expensive, with very little financial aid available. Lists of private schools that offer a postgraduate year can be found online using a search engine.

What Parents Can Do

As your gifted student approaches adolescence and high school, you may become increasingly concerned about achievement. Simultaneously, your child may experience internal and external conflicts while attempting to establish a separate identity. You can help by creating and maintaining a mutually respectful atmosphere, helping your child establish effective priorities, and defining sensible guidelines. There are many instances where we know a great deal more than our students and tell them so. But it may be much better to have a respectful conversation, gently guiding students, even when we think we know best. With that in mind, the following suggestions may be useful:

» A student who experiences a sudden academic decline in one or two subjects during the junior or senior year is probably not an underachiever. This student, however, will need to explain the drop in grades on a college application. When it is handled properly, such an event may be turned into an asset. This idea will be discussed in more detail in Chapter 5.

» Talk about the future on a regular basis. Instead of talking about the need to be admitted to a good college, talk to your child about life beyond the undergraduate years. Discuss the joys and downsides of your own career. Encourage your child to form some ideas about his or her own future.

» Some students are more interested in learning than in working for grades. Such a student might spend hours on a project that is unrelated to academic classes and fail to turn in required work. This inner-directed student should be strongly encouraged to pursue his or her interests, particularly because those interests often lead to lifelong career satisfaction. Simultaneously, the student should be reminded that teachers might be unsympathetic when required work is incomplete. Comprehensive career planning emphasizing short- and long-term goals often helps such a student to complete required assignments, pass high school courses, and plan for college.

» Help kids develop coping strategies. They should know how to deal with setbacks, stresses, and feelings of inadequacy. They should also learn how to solve problems and resolve conflicts, and learn ways to brainstorm and think critically.

» Provide an accepting environment, positive feedback, reasonable rules and guidelines, strong support, and encouragement by recognizing effort, progress, and improvement. Avoid overemphasizing achievement.

» Maintain your objectivity and sense of humor. Parental caring, understanding, and objectivity are critical resources for gifted students to be used as armor when faced with insensitive people.

» Listen to your gifted student. Show genuine interest in his or her observations, interests, activities, and goals. Be sensitive to problems, but avoid transmitting unrealistic or conflicting expectations and solving problems the student is capable of managing.

» Guide your adolescent toward activities and goals that reflect his or her values, interests, and needs, not yours.

» Encourage your student to acquire a wide variety of experiences, particularly those that will assist him or her in college and career planning. For example, if your son is interested in politics, suggest that he volunteer to work in a campaign office. Your child may benefit from such an experience in two ways: (1) by feeling useful for providing a service to the community without thought of compensation; and (2) by knowing and understanding a realistic view of the work world.

» Share your perspective on how you successfully handle stressful situations, disappointment, and discouragement. Underachieving gifted students are frequently idealistic and believe that no one else shares their problems.

» Get involved in your child's school. Volunteer your time. Although your student may be less than appreciative, counselors and teachers need and value your assistance and support. You may also acquire useful information that will help you assist your adolescent.

Search for a group of parents who can provide a support system. Parent advocacy groups for gifted students exist in many communities and offer a network for communication, information, and assistance. In lieu of a local group, contact Supporting Emotional Needs of the Gifted [SENG], a national support group that offers a newsletter and other publications, webinars (online classes), opportunities to communicate with other parents who share the challenges of parenting a gifted teen, and local conferences for parents. Contact them at http://www.sengifted.org. Here are some guidelines to remember in parenting gifted teens:

> » Avoid overinvesting in your child's achievement level.
> » Avoid discouraging comments, such as "If you're so gifted, why did you get a D in _____ ?" or "I've given you everything; why are you so _____ ?"
> » Keep in mind that some students are extremely unhappy in secondary school and do not do well academically (in part because of the organization and structure). These students, however, may handle independence quite well; they may be extremely happy and successful in the right college when learning in an environment with a different structural organization.
> » Some students are underachievers because they do not have the opportunity to use what they know. This is frequently true of musicians and students with technical abilities. If this describes your teen, find an environment where he or she will feel successful.
> » Search for appropriate summer activities that the student will enjoy, particularly those that deal with the student's interests. Some underachieving gifted students develop a love of learning through summer courses and activities, and the love of learning, unlike grades, lasts a lifetime.
> » Provide appropriate college and career guidance by exposing your teen to work environments. Internships usually work well if the student has control over the place and time he works. Some students benefit from a residential college planning seminar offered by many colleges.
> » Avoid praise and artificial compliments. These comments may not resonate with the way the student feels internally. Recognize effort and improvement rather than the final product.

» In college planning, the role of the student and the role of the parent are complementary. They are different yet depend on one another to achieve a positive outcome.

ADDITIONAL READINGS AND RESOURCES

The Connie Belin & Jacqueline N. Blank International Center for Gifted Education and Talent Development. (n.d.). *The paradox of giftedness and autism (PDF)*. Iowa City: The University of Iowa College of Education.

The DukeTIP Digest of Gifted Research. (July, 2013.) Advocating for your gifted child with autism. Retrieved from http://www.tip.duke.edu/node/84.

National Education Association. (2006). *The twice-exceptional dilemma*. Retrieved from http://www. nea.org/assets/docs/twiceexceptional.pdf

Rosenberg, N. (July 2006). The college search process for GT/LD students. *2e Newsletter*. Retrieved from http://www.davidsongifted.org/db/Articles_id_10444.aspx

Simpson, C., & Spencer, V. (2009). College success for students with learning disabilities. Waco, TX: Prufrock Press.

Solow, R., & Rhodes, C. (2012). *College at 13: Young, gifted, and purposeful*. Tucson, AZ: Gifted Potential Press.

Warshaw, M. (2006 July). Helping 2e kids in the transition to college. *2e Newsletter*. Retrieved from http://www.davidsongifted.org/db/Articles_id_10432.aspx

Webb, J. (2013a). *Searching for meaning: idealism, bright minds, disillusionment, and hope*. Tucson, AZ: Great Potential Press.

Wessling, Suki (Nov 1, 2012). *From school to homeschool: Should you homeschool your gifted child?* Tucson, AZ: Great Potential Press.

3 THE COLLEGE SEARCH
A Matter of Matching

College planning for gifted students is about making a match between the gifted student's goals, interests, and needs and a college's offerings. Most of this chapter is written for and to parents because they have a unique perspective. Most parents know their kids, even better than teens know themselves. We can see with a telescope. We see long-term goals, not just short-term objectives. Finding colleges that are "a good fit," rather than "the best college," is a teenager's job. The process will build decision-making skills, analytic skills, and skills in taking responsibility for one's life. However, the part played by parents—(1) investigating possibilities such as competitions, special programs, or classes, and (2) encouraging (cheerleading when necessary)—are critical to success.

Knowing oneself is a critical part of that matching process. When your adolescent begins to compile a list of colleges for consideration, usually sometime during 11th grade, his or her self-knowledge and experiences should govern the choices. Although that sounds like conventional wisdom, most students make arbitrary decisions about college, in part because they don't know what they want and don't know how to find out. They don't realize that colleges vary by size, location, student diversity, extracurricular activities, and programs of study.

Many teens have not reflected on their strengths, interests, and needs. Before making that all-important list of colleges, chosen because they are a match for interests and preferences, your adolescent should begin to answer these questions.

» Who am I—what are my values, attitudes, beliefs, interests?

» What's important to me—family, career, religion, power, money, social life, music, arts, sports?

» Where do I want to live for 4 years—large city, suburbs, rural area?

» Which academic subjects do I like best and least?

» How do I learn best—reading, talking, independently, self-paced, seminar, lecture, hands-on?

» Why do I want to go to college?

The last question may be the most important. A student who wants to party should probably apply to a school that is very different from the student who wants to study with a well-known professor. A student who is passionate about English literature may choose a school that is very different from the one chosen by a computer wizard who wants to specialize in microbiology. The student questionnaire in Figure 2 gives students an idea of the type of college they should look for.

KNOWING ONESELF

The years from the beginning of high school to the end of 12th grade are turbulent times for all adolescents, particularly gifted adolescents. During this critical period, your child will try on many personalities that will blend into his or her self-awareness. Hopefully, your teen will learn to use talents in constructive, satisfying ways, and develop an appreciation for his or her community. Your child needs to discover, explore, investigate, and participate in different types of activities, intellectual ideas, academic disciplines, extracurricular activities, and social

Many colleges and universities offer a well-rounded education, an escape from home, and the time and opportunity to pursue abilities and interests. But, if you take a closer look at why you are going to college, you will get a better idea of how selective you should be in your search. There are 25 statements listed below. Check off the 5 statements that most accurately describe your reasons for going to college. They are not listed in any particular order.

My reasons for going to college include:

_____ 1. To live in a different part of the country.

_____ 2. To be exposed to new ideas.

_____ 3. To have a more interesting social life.

_____ 4. To be near cultural activities.

_____ 5. To get practical experience in my chosen field.

_____ 6. To prepare for a specific professional school (e.g., law, architecture, dentistry, or medicine).

_____ 7. To get a solid liberal arts background.

_____ 8. To participate in athletic activities.

_____ 9. To be challenged academically.

_____ 10. To compete with others on my level.

_____ 11. To go to a high-status school.

_____ 12. To get specific vocational or career training.

_____ 13. To help me get a good job or career.

_____ 14. To meet people different from myself.

_____ 15. To study and live abroad.

_____ 16. To take classes from renowned professors.

_____ 17. To develop my abilities, potential, talents, and interests.

_____ 18. To participate in a special educational program.

_____ 19. To be out on my own.

_____ 20. To join in extracurricular activities.

Figure 2. Why are you going to college?

_____ 21. To earn a better living and have a better lifestyle.

_____ 22. To satisfy my parents.

_____ 23. To go where my friends are going.

_____ 24. Because I have nothing better to do.

_____ 25. To have fun and not work too hard for the next 2 to 4 years.

If you checked off numbers 2, 3, 8, 17, 19, 22, 24, or 25, almost any college can offer you the right opportunities. If you chose numbers 1, 4, 5, 7, 9, 10, 12, 13, 14, 15, 18, 20, 21, or 23, you will have to be more selective. If numbers 6, 11, or 16 were among your choices, you will have to look for a highly competitive and academically prestigious school.

Figure 2. Continued.

relationships. To accomplish this, he or she should be exposed to and participate in many different types of activities. Middle school and high school are meant for exploration, growing intellectually, finding interests and passions, and learning to accept challenges. It is also important for your child to begin to develop effective writing skills, which will prove essential in high school and college. Students learn a great deal about themselves each time they participate in anything new and develop new skills.

Understanding oneself depends, in part, on one's breadth and depth of experience, because it is through experience that we know what we like and what we dislike. This section of the book includes many different types of academic and nonacademic opportunities that will send your child on an exploratory journey toward an expanding self-awareness. Almost any activity can be a source of enrichment for your son or daughter. However, a highly enriching activity will bring some intrinsic, as well as extrinsic rewards in the form of self-confidence and a growing sense of self. Summer is an opportunity for out-of-school enrichment and should not be spent frivolously. It is usually the most convenient time your teen can take a course and investigate new topics. Colleges are very interested in how adolescents spend their free time, because it's one way to tell the difference between two equally deserving candidates in a competitive environment. An unchallenging summer activity is not going to impress colleges. However, if a college admissions reader sees that your child spent his or her free time wisely—learning new skills, sharing talents compassionately, and exhibiting leadership—the reader is likely to award extra points. However, if the reader sees that a child spent the summer acquiring a suntan, the candidate becomes less appealing.

Self-Knowledge Goals

The ingredients of self-knowledge for adolescents are reflective self-exploration, academic planning, intellectual and social/emotional enrichment, decision-making skills (how to analyze and evaluate alternatives), and effective work and study skills, including time management. Before students reach the active portion of college planning, the part that involves looking at colleges, they should know something about their interests and, in particular, what they want from a college. The questionnaire in Figure 2 will help determine that. The answers may change as students get older, and that's OK.

Many students have not thought about what truly interests them. Of course, interests change as we age, but knowing and pursuing the topics and activities that interest you can help you shape your future. Having your child complete an interest inventory is a way for him to start thinking about how his interests relate to his future.

SOURCES OF ENRICHMENT AND SUMMER OPPORTUNITIES

Does your son or daughter have a passion to work side by side with a microbiologist 8 hours a day, or collaborate with playwrights and directors to produce a new play? Be immersed in the world of music? Write for 12 hours a day, creating short stories, poems, essays, or a weekly newspaper? Study the ecosystems of coral reefs on daily dives in the Caribbean? Build a wooden sea kayak and paddle it along the Maine coast for 3 weeks? Learn to speak Arabic, Chinese, or Portuguese? These are all possible pursuits during the summer months. Summer is the time when teenagers can learn new skills, add to a repertoire, and if she is lucky, add to a resume. Summer is the time to explore and discover new activities or polish the old. There are hundreds of activities to try and summer is the time.

During the next few years, there is likely to be a time when your gifted child wants to learn something entirely new, like psychology, creative writing, archaeology, or genealogy. A typical school day does not leave time for exploring a topic in depth, or playing with ideas. Most teachers follow a state-approved syllabus, which can be very confining. If your child is gifted but does not participate in a gifted program, he or she may have few true peers. Finding an appropriate summer enrichment opportunity might provide a good solution. There are literally hundreds of places to look for enrichment. Every state has a university that offers enrichment to high school students during the summer. The regional talent search programs are a good source, as is your own school district. Lots of school districts offer fee-based summer enrichment classes. Some school districts sponsor overseas travel. Teenagers should stretch during the summer.

We live in a world where there is so much to do that it's sometimes hard to decide what we want. We have a lot of choices, as do our children. Do we want to improve skills? Develop new skills? Help someone less fortunate?

Some gifted students tend to take on too many activities and commitments. As a parent, you can tell when your child is overextended and stressed, and if you see that happening during the summer, eliminate some activities so that your child has less to cope with. This does not mean that students should be encouraged to devote their summer months to catching up on soap operas or mastering the newest video game—just that they should do something stimulating and interesting, look for a change of pace, *and* take time to relax. Colleges and future employers like to see creativity, compassion, and leadership.

Parents and students should consider the following questions when discussing enrichment opportunities:

» What are the adolescent's intellectual, social, and emotional needs?

» How does a particular enrichment opportunity match those needs?

» What new opportunities will benefit your teen and what does he or she want to do?

» How does the cost of a program compare to the services and resources provided, and is scholarship money available from the program or outside organizations?

For lists and descriptions of enrichment programs for gifted and talented students, see *Educational Opportunity Guide: A Directory of Programs for the Gifted* (available at http://www.duketipeog.com/guide/search), or my book, *The Best Summer Programs for Teens* (Berger, 2013). The National Association for Gifted Children (NAGC) also provides a searchable database of summer programs (http://nagc.org/SummerPrograms.aspx). Pre-College Programs: Find the Right Pre-College Summer Programs (available at http://www.petersons.com/college-search/summer-programs-camps-search.aspx), lists almost 3,000 national and international summer programs, tours, and service projects.

When using some lists, keep in mind that to be included, programs must pay a fee, which may limit some programs from participating.

Above-Grade-Level Testing

Above-grade-level testing means taking a standardized test that is meant for considerably older students. Young students may find it valuable to assess their abilities compared with much older students. The major college entrance tests are the SAT and ACT, which are both frequently taken by seventh- and eighth-grade students. Some talent search programs offer standardized tests geared to students who are younger than seventh grade, such as the EXPLORE test of the American College Testing (ACT) program and the PLUS test of the Educational Testing Service (ETS). Both tests may offer students a way of understanding their intellectual and academic strengths and weaknesses and give them time to improve their weaker areas before reaching high school. Information about either of these tests is available from your closest regional talent search program or ACT and ETS.

Regional Talent Searches and Cooperative Programs

The term *talent search* refers to a specific type of educational program for gifted and advanced learners held within the United States. All of the talent searches are located regionally; their service areas range from single-state searches to quite large ones. The largest regional talent search programs are the Center for Talented Youth at Johns Hopkins University (CTY), the Talent Identification Program at Duke University (TIP), the Northwestern University Center for Talent Development (CTD), and the Western Academic Talent Search (WATS) at the Center for Bright Kids. Although the four programs have unique features, each conducts its talent search in basically the same way. Seventh- and eighth-grade students who score at the 95th percentile or above on a standardized achievement test register to take the SAT or the ACT in the fall. The talent search programs use the SAT and ACT because they provide a better measure of intellectual abilities than standardized achievement tests designed for the middle school level. Participating in the testing can provide the young teen with an assessment of his or her abilities compared with those of students who are high school juniors or seniors. (The scores of students who are below ninth grade are not reported to colleges when you take the tests later, unless you choose to do so.) Based on students' scores on the SAT or ACT, various kinds of educational options and experiences, ranging from high-level enrichment courses to subject and grade acceleration, are recommended.

The talent search includes three important components: (1) diagnosis and evaluation of levels of talent; (2) educational placement and guidance; and (3) talent development opportunities including summer programs, distance learning programs, contests, and competitions.

Qualified students may be invited to participate in summer residential programs or commuter programs or take advantage of other academic opportunities. The programs also offer college and career planning assistance. Talent search opportunities have taken many different forms: fast-paced summer classes and Saturday programs, early access to AP courses, enrollment of junior high students in high school courses, dual enrollment of high school students in college classes, correspondence courses for high school and college-level courses, and early entrance programs for college. Each of the four universities that conduct a regional talent search produces a compendium of educational programs within its region, and the number of programs grows annually.

An outgrowth of the regional talent search is the Elementary Student Talent Search (for grades 3–6), offered by Carnegie Mellon University, Northwestern University, the University of Iowa, and Duke University, as well as the Young Students Talent Search (grades 5 and 6) offered by Johns Hopkins University. The requirements for participation include scoring at the 95th percentile on grade-level standardized tests.

The goals of all of the programs include the following:

» to identify academically talented young people,

» to inform them of their abilities and academic options,

» to sponsor challenging educational programs, and

» to develop an effective research effort to help understand the nature of academically talented adolescents (Johns Hopkins University Center for Talented Youth, n.d.).

Additional goals and specific provisions depend on the individual program.

Courses offered by talent search programs are specifically designed to challenge students with high ability. Directors of national talent searches point out the following intellectual and social/emotional advantages of these programs:

» Students who tend to concentrate on specific academic disciplines (e.g., mathematics and science) are encouraged to explore previously undiscovered disciplines such as philosophy, anthropology, or psychology.

» Students who require academic acceleration can choose from a wide variety of courses that might not be available in their local high schools.

» Students establish and maintain relationships with other adolescents who share their abilities, views, and interests. This is particularly important for gifted students, because they frequently feel isolated.

» Students receive information on college and career planning.

» Students who have participated in regional talent search programs and other university-based institutes say that friendships established during the summer continue years later.

Why should students participate in talent searches? Talent searches provide students with a better measure of their abilities, allow them to become eligible for educational opportunities (such as summer classes, informational mailings, and career symposia), and provide them with information that is useful in educational placement and guidance.

If your student is eligible for educational opportunities and summer enrichment through a regional talent search or other organization, keep in mind that participation in the program is not required. You can simply say to yourself, "Now I know that he or she is eligible" and drop the idea. However, if your teen participates and takes a course that might require a high school schedule change, you should tell the high school before they make up student schedules. For example, if your student takes algebra during the summer and will require geometry in the fall, don't wait until the last minute to tell your child's guidance counselor.

Governor's School Programs

Governor's School residential programs provide intensive high-quality programs that focus on diverse areas (e.g., arts or academic disciplines such as science). Many states offer a residential Governor's School program only to students who are between their junior and senior year. Specific criteria for selection of students differ, depending on the state. In some states, local educators nominate students, but in many states, a student may inform a teacher or guidance counselor that he or she wants to be considered for nomination. In other states, students may contact the program directly and request nomination. Specific program goals also vary by state, but all programs recognize academic excellence and artistic or leadership ability. For general information about Governor's Schools, visit the National Conference of Governor's Schools website at http://ncogs.org.

Mentor Relationships

One of the most valuable experiences a high school student can have is exposure to a mentor who is willing to share his or her personal values, particular interests, time, talents, and skills.

When the mentor is a good match for your child, the relationship can provide both your son or daughter and his or her mentor with encouragement, inspiration, new insights, and other personal rewards. Many students find mentors while participating in talent search programs or high school internships. Internships are valuable because they allow a student to investigate a potential career interest. A mentorship, on the other hand, is a relationship in which values, attitudes, passions, and traditions are passed from one person to another and internalized.

The benefits of having a mentor ultimately affect a student's choice of career and salary. In terms of career advancement, particularly for women, mentors make a huge difference. Presidential Scholars are selected from the brightest 12th-grade students in the nation. In a study of Presidential Scholars 15 years after these students graduated from high school, they were asked questions that pertained to the nature, role, and influence of their most significant mentors. Although not everyone had a mentor, those who did said that having a role model, and the support and encouragement of a mentor were the biggest benefits (Kaufmann, 1981; Kaufmann, Harrel, Milam, Woolverton, & Miller, 1986). Mentors set an example, offered intellectual stimulation, communicated excitement and joy in the learning process, and understood these students and their needs.

The research also revealed the critical importance of mentors for gifted girls (Kaufmann et al., 1986). In this study, the earning power of the women and men was compared, and it was discovered that there was a salary gap between men and women in the same profession who shared the same credentials. The men were paid more for the same work. However, when the earning powers of the women were equal to those of the men, it was discovered that those women had had one or more mentors. In other words, the presence of a mentor may equalize earning power (Kaufmann, 1981; Kaufmann et al., 1986).

Educators, counselors, and parents can all help gifted students find mentors. The following questions may help you decide whether to pursue this approach.

» Does the student want a mentor? Or, does the student simply want exposure to a particular subject or career field?
» Is the student prepared to spend a significant amount of time working with the mentor?
» Does the student understand the purpose, benefits, and limitations of the mentor relationship?

To identify mentor candidates, contact local businesses, universities, professional associations, and organizations such as the American Association of Retired Persons. Your child may want to focus on working on a significant and specific project with his or her mentor. Such projects can later be submitted for recognition by competitions and contests, and the experience of working on the project can also provide a valuable asset in college applications, essays, and interviews.

If you can identify some mentor candidates, you may want to ask the following questions:

» Does the mentor understand and like working with gifted adolescents?
» Is the mentor willing to be a real role model, sharing the excitement and joy of learning?
» Is the mentor's teaching style compatible with the student's learning style?

Community Service and Volunteer Activities

Students need to learn how to share their talents freely with others. When we help others, we learn much about ourselves and make our own lives more meaningful. This can be accomplished in many ways. You might suggest that your student volunteer at a local nursing home or a hospital, or share a specific talent with young children. For example, teens can coach a local children's athletic team or teach computer programming to low-income students. The focus of the volunteer work will depend on your child's talent and available resources. Your teen's school might

67

institute a volunteer program, such as the one held annually at a Virginia magnet school, which helps its students find opportunities to share their talents. At the Virginia school, community service is a graduation requirement. A wide variety of activities are offered, and the students are highly enthusiastic about their service opportunities. They volunteer for activities such as tutoring younger children, reading to older persons, and participating in political campaigns. Students can also learn about many careers by volunteering their time to businesses and nonprofit organizations.

Travel

There are many significant benefits to exposing your child to other environments and cultures, in the U.S. or in other countries. School systems throughout the nation sponsor overseas travel during the summer, preceded by several weeks of classes in which students absorb some of the history and culture of the country where they plan to travel. Selected teachers and parents often serve as chaperones. If classes are offered prior to and following summer travel, students are introduced to the country to be visited and encouraged to discuss their experiences when they return. One teenager used part of his college application to talk about participating in an archeological dig, studying the lab techniques, and learning how to look for relics. He particularly enjoyed squeezing through tunnels a few meters below the surface, finding pottery or different relics.

ADVANCED ACADEMICS

Although colleges are concerned with the outside enrichment opportunities a student undertakes to explore interests, their primary concern remains the student's ability to be successful under stressful, challenging academic conditions. Taking challenging advanced-level classes is a good way to show colleges and yourself that you are ready for college-level work.

Some gifted students will be attracted to highly selective colleges, schools that reject more applications than they accept. The most selective colleges look for evidence of high student motivation and achievement—good grades in very demanding courses. They expect to see AP or IB courses on the student's transcript, if these courses are provided by the student's high school. Planning for advanced courses must begin as early as the eighth or ninth grade, especially in the case of sequential courses such as mathematics. For instance, the progression to AP Calculus requires several years of prerequisite courses beginning with algebra. The same kind of planning is necessary for languages and sciences. Some students will not be ready or able to begin an advanced mathematics, foreign language, or science sequence by eighth grade. In such cases, courses offered during the summer or correspondence courses sponsored by regional talent search programs may be a viable option that allows the student to catch up with peers.

Advanced Placement Courses

AP courses offer gifted high school students the opportunity to broaden their depth and scope of learning in one or more subjects of interest, pursue college-level studies while still enrolled in secondary school, and demonstrate their capacity to handle college-level work. Students enrolled in AP courses may develop study skills that match or exceed those of college freshmen. To earn college credit, students take the AP Examination, a 3-hour comprehensive test in an individual subject area. Good exam results can be parlayed into college credits and permissions to advance directly to higher level courses. However, college admissions staff members are rarely impressed with a grade of B or less and AP test scores of 1 or 2 out of 5. In a recent blog (Abrams, 2013a), a dean of admission discussed "what admissions officers look for when reviewing a student's transcript, how students should balance rigorous classes and extracurricular activities, and whether it's better to have an A in an honors class or a B in an Advanced Placement class" (para. 4).

His response was, "The student should take the most challenging course that is best for him or her. The extra challenge of the AP course may prepare the student better for the challenge of college courses" (para. 20). In other words, if a student's high school offers advanced classes, admissions staff members expect to see them. On the other hand, staff members would prefer to see straight A's over straight B's and C's. The choice belongs with the student. B's may not get you into a top tier college, but a second tier school might immediately recognize you as a match.

Students must choose carefully when taking the exams. A fee is charged for each test, and studying for AP tests takes a lot of time. They should know what they would gain from taking each test (College Board, n.d.a). If they are already taking three or four exams, perhaps taking that fifth exam may not make sense.

When looking at colleges, students should keep in mind that some colleges offer exemption, credit, or both for AP Exam grades of 3, 4, or 5. Because high schools calculate a student's overall GPA in different ways, many colleges recalculate the GPA, often taking into account the academic rigor of the courses on a transcript. If a student is seriously interested in a college, she should investigate course credit and placement.

AP Exams are offered each May at participating schools to students who want to be tested at the college level in areas such as English, calculus, science, computer science, history, foreign languages, art, and music. AP courses and examinations now cover more than 35 subjects, including art history, economics (micro and macro), and studio art (2-D and 3-D design), and they are taken by more than two million students from more than 18,000 schools, including those in other countries (College Board, 2012). A student need not be enrolled in an AP course in order to take the exam. AP tests are graded on a scale from 1 to 5 (5 is the highest score). Exemption or AP credit varies among colleges and is offered at the discretion of each college. AP scores are usually available online in July of every year.

Some states receive a grant to enable them to reimburse low-income individuals for part or all of the cost of AP test fees if those low-income individuals (a) are enrolled in an AP class, and (b) plan to take an AP test. Contact your state education agency or board of education for more information.

Each college or university decides how much credit, if any, will be awarded to the student depending on the test score. Many highly selective colleges will accept only a score of 5 for credit. To find colleges that offer AP credit or placement, visit the College Board's website (http://www.collegeboard.com). If a student takes an AP test, the student is responsible for ensuring that the scores reach the college. For additional information about AP Programs, visit the College Board's AP Central (College Board AP Central, n.d.; http://apcentral.collegeboard.com).

The College Board provides broad outlines of course content and examination methods. However, the specific curriculum content of AP courses is determined by each school or school district and taught by high school teachers. This means that there will be some inconsistencies in the quality of courses and the preparedness of teachers, although everyone takes the same AP exam in a specific topic.

Apex Learning (http://www.apexlearning.com/) offers online courses designed by teachers familiar with AP curriculum requirements. An online AP instructor and up to 25 students interact via online discussion groups, chats, and e-mail. Each course includes online curricula, activities on CD-ROM, reading materials, and access to Apex's AP Exam Review in the spring. Pennsylvania Homeschoolers (http://www.aphomeschoolers.com/) offers online AP courses to homeschooled students worldwide. Most of the talent search programs also offer online AP courses and examinations. For example, additional services offered by Duke TIP can be found at http://www.tip.duke.edu/loyo/overview_large_9.27.06.pdf.

Honors Versus Advanced Placement Courses

Many secondary schools throughout the country offer both an AP program and an honors program. Because students often have to choose between the programs, it's important for parents, as well as students, to understand the difference.

The AP Program consists of courses in a wide variety of subject areas developed by both high school and college faculty under the auspices of the College Board. The courses cover the breadth of information, skills, and assignments found in corresponding college courses. Most U.S. colleges and universities, as well as colleges and universities in 28 other countries, have an AP policy granting incoming students credit, placement, or both on the basis of their grades on AP Exams. Many of these institutions grant up to a full year of college credit (sophomore standing) to students who earn a sufficient number of qualifying AP grades. There have been several research studies that looked at what students gain by taking an AP course and taking an AP exam. It makes sense that students who take the course and score well on the exam have a better chance at succeeding in college and graduating on time, in 4 years (Mollison, 2006). But, what about the students who take the course, take the exam, and do not score well? Surprisingly, researchers have discovered that even these students benefit from the rigor in studying for the exam. It's possible that the effort prepares them for college examinations, even though they did not score well (Mathews, 2005).

Honors classes differ from AP courses in several ways. First, they are developed locally by district teachers to meet the needs of high-achieving students. Second, most honors classes offer the same curriculum offered in the corresponding regular, non-honors classes at the school, but the honors classes are designed to be more challenging by covering additional topics or some topics in greater depth. Most students and parents want to know whether AP courses are more difficult than honors classes. The answer is usually yes; however, "difficult" is a relative concept, so the answer really depends on the nature of the honors courses and the standards upheld in those courses.

Students should understand that unlike AP courses, honors courses won't earn them college credit, but there are still important benefits. For example, colleges will recognize a student's willingness to challenge himself academically. Honors courses also prepare students for college-level work. Be sure that your child's high school transcripts indicate a course as honors—particularly if it's not part of the transcript course description—so colleges easily recognize honors courses students have taken.

The benefits of advanced-level courses outweigh the drawbacks. Some of the advantages are more far-reaching than simply making your child more appealing to prospective colleges. Some high schools award extra credit to students who take AP courses.

The International Baccalaureate (IB) Program

The International Baccalaureate (IB) Organization's Diploma Programme, created in 1968, is a comprehensive and challenging preuniversity course that demands the best from motivated students and teachers. This sophisticated curriculum covers a wide range of academic subjects and has stood the test of more than 500,000 students in 119 countries since 1968. The world's leading universities welcome IB graduates because the rigor of the curriculum is well-known. Diploma candidates are required to undertake original research and write an extended essay of about 4,000 words. This project offers the opportunity to investigate a topic of special interest and acquaints students with the kind of independent research and writing skills expected at a university. Students who graduate from the program may earn college credit or advanced standing at many colleges or universities (Boyd, 1999). The IB lists college recognition policies and gives other information on its website (http://www.ibo.org).

The IB offers three programmes of international education and a career-related certificate. Although the IB now offers a sequence of three programmes—the Primary Year Programme

(PYP, for students aged 3 to 12), the Middle Years Programme (MYP, designed for students aged 11 to 16), and the Diploma Programme (DP, designed for students aged 16 to 19)—each programme must continue to be self-contained, since the IB has no requirement for schools to offer more than one programme. However, they must also form an articulated sequence for those schools that teach all three programmes or any sequence of two.

EARLY ENTRANCE TO COLLEGE

Some gifted adolescents have a difficult time with the organizational patterns and the ordinary pace of secondary school education, even while taking advanced courses. Impatient with a secondary school system and an academic structure that does not meet their needs, they accelerate their courses to leave high school early. Most colleges will take students who have completed 3 years of high school. However, many colleges are reluctant to accept younger students without evidence of emotional maturity. Early entrance programs (listed in Appendix A) can provide a combined high school and college curriculum that may be more appropriate for extraordinarily gifted young people. In such programs, these students may, for the first time, find true peers, or others who share their passion for learning. In the words of one student who enrolled in the PEG program, "Suddenly, I wasn't just passing time until my real life began. My life developed purpose and direction" (Solow & Rhodes, 2012, p. 87).

Students who are eligible for and want to be radically accelerated (that is, accelerated more than one grade) need to think about early entrance in terms of what they will miss if they skip 2 or more years of high school. This needs to be a family decision, in part because families will incur college expenses before they are ready. There are fewer scholarships available to underage students than there are for students who enter "on time." However, there are advantages as well (Robinson & Davidson Institute, 2005). Students who love learning, feel a hunger to acquire a deeper understanding of the world, and enjoy communicating in writing may find a more compatible fit in college. Students who expect a long educational path to a career may want to get an early start. For example, students who know they will need multiple degrees (e.g., both an M.D. and a Ph.D.) can expect to attend school for many years. For profoundly gifted students, early entrance may not be the solution to every problem, but it may be a better fit than high school.

The disadvantages of early entrance should be recognized and discussed. If high school sports, music, journalism, or any other high school activity that is important to a student will be hard to give up, then high school may be a better fit, at least for a while. Young students might find that they are the youngest on campus, and need to stay at home while attending college. These students may miss out on some of the most significant college experiences and bonding that takes place when students live together away from home. The various options and alternatives (e.g., taking online courses, competitions, AP or IB classes) should be discussed with the entire family, because when a young student attends college, the entire family feels the impact (Robinson & Davidson Institute, 2005). Talking to other students who have chosen early entrance and reading guidebooks and other information on the topic may help students and families to think through the options (Solow & Rhodes, 2012).

DEVELOPING A PLAN

Every gifted student should be strongly encouraged by the end of eighth grade to develop a 4-year academic plan that includes academic courses required for graduation and courses desired for college planning. The plan should also include how a student will manage time, showing the hours he or she will spend in academic high school classes, in extracurricular activities, doing homework, and the hours needed for family activities, rest, and relaxation. When time is planned carefully, and when

75

plans are monitored and reviewed annually, students learn how to manage their time effectively and how to set priorities.

Effective Work/Study Skills and Time Management

Some kids find it especially difficult to manage their time. They start a project and lose track of time. They are so intensely focused that they honestly don't hear you when you call them to dinner for the third time. When a child is so interested and stimulated by the world, school projects and afterschool programs can easily become overwhelming. Highly motivated minds often strive for perfection, leading many gifted kids to overcommit themselves and eventually feel burned out. You are your child's best resource, so become a time management expert now, and launch a smooth back-to-school routine. Keep track of what works and what doesn't, so you can launch into a successful routine every year until your children go to college or leave home. Managing time well is the most significant way in which effective and ineffective students differ from one another (Robinson & Davidson Institute, 2005).

Many students are able to breeze though school, taking on new classes and activities with barely a thought. School is relatively easy for them, so there has been no need for these students to learn to study effectively or manage their time wisely. These students often underestimate how much time will be needed to do homework in a demanding program. When truly challenged late in high school or in college, they may discover that they do not have the skills needed to organize, study, and produce high-quality work. By the time they graduate from high school, students should have some idea as to how to study in different ways for different academic subjects and different types of assessments.

Helping adolescents manage their time depends in large part on their thinking style. Some students are systematic; they keep neat notebooks and like to organize. Their desks and lockers have a place for everything, with similar items grouped together. They usually take tests well, especially when these tests have multiple-choice questions. Other students are more creative and organize differently. The following sections will give students a jumping off point for learning to effectively and proactively manage their time.

One way to manage your time is to set up a time management chart, delegating specific amounts of your time each week to certain activities, like school, sleep, and practice. At the beginning of the school year, try to break down your time each week according to each activity. Record those breakdowns on a chart like the one in Figure 3. Each time you want to add an activity, or if you find your activities are taking up more or less time than you set aside, go back to the chart and readjust your figures. You can trade out activities (such as talking on the phone or surfing the Internet) for others (such as a once-in-a-lifetime concert or attending your school's fall football games). When you have major school projects or assignments, predict how long the assignment will take by breaking it down into steps, allotting amounts of time for specific tasks (e.g., 2 hours to write the first draft, an hour for revisions, etc.). Then, determine if you need to schedule more time for homework each week until the project is completed. You may want to consider setting aside a particular time to work on organizing your chart each week or month. Keeping an up-to-date, thorough time management chart will help you make the most of your time, enjoy the activities you want to take part in, and ensure that your responsibilities, like finishing your homework or writing those college essays, get done.

Another way to think about time management is to create pictures. This is good for students who are visual learners. Make a time chart that looks like a favorite food or topic. For example, picture a multilayered hamburger (see Figure 4). The meat is at the center. What does the meat represent? School? Home? Let's say that the meat represents school or learning. In a 24-hour day, how much lettuce, cheese, or ketchup will you need? Is cheese the homework? Is the sauce your free time? Any image will work

The following chart shows the way you spend your time during an average week on various activities. If it does not include everything you do, be sure to add in activities or you won't get a realistic picture of your time. Estimate the amount of time spent on each item. Once you have this amount, multiply it by the number indicated (some questions do not require multiplication). This will give you the total time spent on the activity in 1 week. After each item's weekly time has been calculated, add all of these times together for the grand total. Subtract this from 168, the total possible hours per week. The remaining hours are the hours you have allowed yourself to study. If you have zero hours to study, go back and see what you can cut down or eliminate.

1. Number of hours of sleep each night:

   _____ x 7 = _____

2. Number of grooming hours per day:

   _____ x 7 = _____

3. Number of hours for meals/snacks per day—include preparation time:

   _____ x 7 = _____

4. Total travel time to and from school on weekdays:

   _____ x 5 = _____

5. Number of hours per week for regularly scheduled functions (music lessons, sports, family chores, religious school, babysitting, etc.):

   _____

6. Number of hours per week for scheduled extracurricular activities:

   _____

7. Number of hours per day for chores, errands, etc.:

   _____ x 7 = _____

Figure 3. Time management chart.

---

8. Number of hours spent in school per day:

    _____ x 5 = _____

9. Number of average hours per week socializing on the phone or with friends:

    _____

Now add up the totals: _____

Subtract the above number from 168, the number of hours in a week: 168 - _____ = _____

Figure 3. Continued.

---

as long as it has tiers or pieces that are a different size from one another. This kind of time management may make a lot more sense than a time chart with arbitrary divisions.

Decision-Making Skills

There are some adolescents who make decisions easily and intuitively know how to weigh risks. Decision making is second nature to these adolescents, but needs to be taught to others who may not be able to anticipate outcomes. Your child needs to know how to evaluate choices and alternative solutions, make judgments, and test solutions if she is going to make decisions that are in her best interests—in other words, a game plan. Where college planning is concerned, you can play a large part in helping your child learn to evaluate her decisions. Highly creative students may need to be taught evaluation skills while they are looking at the differences between colleges. These students receive a lot of mail from colleges. If they can't separate what information is useful from what isn't, they might wind up keeping everything and then finding nothing when they need it.

It is especially important to teach decision-making skills to multipotential adolescents who perform well in all academic areas and are involved in a variety of extracurricular activities.

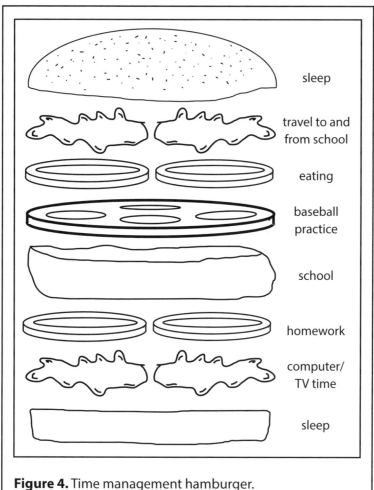

Figure 4. Time management hamburger.

Eventually, they will need to choose areas of concentration and set priorities. Decision-making skills are equally important for students who are highly sensitive to expectations of others, particularly when those expectations conflict with self-fulfillment. Students also need to learn that choosing *not* to decide is a choice that may determine a person's future. They need to be able to connect outcomes with the decisions they make.

A skillful decision maker follows these steps when making decisions:

1. Know something about yourself.
2. Recognize and define the decision to be made (what school courses to take, how to select a college academic major, what colleges or universities to consider).
3. Assess and evaluate the information you have. Decide what facts and ideas are missing.
4. Generate strategies to acquire additional information.
5. Gather additional information, facts, and ideas related to the goal.
6. Assess the advantages, disadvantages, and consequences (risks and costs) of each alternative by asking the following questions:
    *   Will I be satisfied with this choice?
    *   Will I be happy with this choice?
    *   Will others (parents) approve of this choice?
    *   How will I feel about this choice in 6 months? In one year? In 5 years?

7. Make a choice. Write it down. State it aloud. Does it feel right? If the answer is no, repeat the process using another choice.
8. Develop a game plan or strategy to obtain the desired goal.
9. Review the outcome. If it doesn't make sense, begin again. Make sure that the process itself (i.e., following the steps precisely) doesn't get in the way of reaching a decision.
10. Distinguish between decisions and outcomes. (Good decisions can have poor outcomes, and vice versa.)

YOUR CHILD'S GUIDANCE COUNSELOR

Parents should establish and maintain a positive working relationship with their child's guidance counselor in middle school, and particularly in high school. This valuable professional can provide information about curricula, accelerated courses, enrichment classes, summer opportunities, and various educational options. Because the guidance counselor is familiar with the school and home communities, his or her perspective and expertise will prove invaluable when making plans for secondary and undergraduate study. In addition to selecting appropriate, challenging courses, the counselor can recommend programs and resources that will nurture a child's gifts and talents.

Your child's counselor can be their best friend and adviser. However, almost 60% of eighth-grade students in the nation go to high school without having discussed the selection of their courses with a school counselor (Frome & Dunham, 2002). When asked how frequently they met with their guidance counselors, most of the students interviewed for this book responded by saying "Not enough; sometimes once a year, sometimes two or three times."

The average counselor is responsible for anywhere between 500 and 1,000 students, many of whom are experiencing serious personal problems. The gifted students interviewed for this book said that their guidance counselors are doing the best they can, but because they must respond to so many needs, the job seems impossible. It is not surprising, therefore, that our gifted children are reluctant to use a counselor's time to discuss problems or future plans. Some feel their concerns are not nearly as critical as those experienced by other students and, because they are logical people, they can figure out solutions by themselves. Unfortunately, they tend to believe the myth that gifted students can make it on their own.

This year, there are high school seniors all over the U.S. receiving acceptance letters from colleges of their choice and deciding where to enroll in the fall. There are also many high school seniors whose academic achievement places them in the top tiers of the nation, but who will not enroll in college after high school because they are from poor families. What is ironic, according to a study by sociologists at Johns Hopkins University, is that this "talent loss" among students from low-income environments often has relatively little to do with their families' financial wherewithal. Instead, it often occurs because these students never receive practical advice on applying to college from their high school guidance counselors or other adults (Plank & Jordan, 2001). They didn't plan for college well. Many didn't seriously start to look into college until the second semester of their senior year. Often, they hadn't taken the ACTs, SATs, or other achievement tests when they needed to, or they had made poor choices in course selections. A large number didn't know about the availability of financial aid and scholarships and assumed that they couldn't afford college.

As a parent, it is your responsibility to make sure that your child sees a guidance counselor to discuss his or her choice of courses and to develop a 4-year plan. If possible, you should also attend that meeting. And, make sure your child sees the counselor every year, so that by the time the counselor has to write a college recommendation, the counselor will know your teen well enough to describe in detail why he or she will be successful in college. (Chapter 5 includes a form that may help your counselor write a helpful recommendation letter.)

CAREER EXPLORATION

83

> Nothing is so simple for me that I can do a perfect job without effort, but nothing is so hard that I cannot do it. This is why I find it so difficult to decide my place in the future.
> —A gifted student

How does math translate into a career if you don't want to teach math? What kind of preparation do you need for a career as a performing artist or an architect? Why learn history when you know you will never work in a museum or teach history? These are some of the questions adolescents ask. The problems encountered by some students are illustrated by the response to an interview with a 22-year-old multitalented graduate of a prestigious university, who said, "School taught me to make rational choices, but how does a rational mind navigate when options are infinite and nebulous? I need some time to tune my instincts. I need some experiences."

Mentors or internships can fill some of the need for experience. For example, Ashley decided during ninth grade that she wanted to become a talk show host someday. She applied for and was awarded an internship at a local television channel, and spent time there after school for the next few months. During her internship, she saw the less glamorous aspects of being a talk show host and talked to professionals about their schooling. At the end of her internship, she decided that she preferred advertising, and ultimately was highly successful in that field.

It is common to attribute extraordinary powers to gifted students who are preparing for the world of work. Contrary to popular thinking, however, they need special help to prepare for that world, in part because of their characteristics and in part because an occupation often becomes lifelong career development for gifted students. Gifted students need more, not less, information and assistance with career planning, because some have more alternatives than they can realistically consider and some are caught in a conflict between self-fulfillment and pleasing other people. Too often, gifted young people are expected to succeed on their own or adapt to whatever situations they happen to encounter; thus, career planning is left to chance.

Focusing on Your Future

Many colleges and universities hold all-day or longer academic and career planning activities for secondary gifted students, ages 11–16. Students are given opportunities to interact with professionals in varied fields and parents are informed about career-oriented academic planning. College faculty or professionals lead career workshops in the humanities and social sciences, art, mathematics, science, and technology. Parent sessions include topics such as college planning and finances, encouraging girls in math and science, and the social and emotional needs of gifted students.

Career exploration should help students understand the relationship between school and careers, become familiar with realistic career options, set short- and long-term goals, and plan for the future. That is why career exploration is a self-discovery process. Most adolescents don't have a clue as to what they want to do as adults. Some know what they'll do when they are young children, but those students are in the minority. Because technology constantly makes new jobs and careers possible, many of our gifted adolescents will be some of the first to work in their career fields.

When students are not provided with appropriate career planning information in high school, they may choose college majors or careers prematurely and arbitrarily, or delay decision making until well into adulthood.

Gifted high school students take career planning seriously. However, high school teachers barely have time to cover the syllabus and rarely engage in career guidance. Some high schools have career centers, but no adult works in the career center to help students with these decisions. In addition, gifted students tend to change majors at least once during college, and some change majors four or five times, and continue to express uncertainty about career choices later in life (Kaufmann, 1981; Simpson & Kaufmann, 1981).

Career planning based on a student's values, interests, needs, and personal cognitive style, as opposed to aptitudes and abilities, seems to be more effective than traditional methods for youngsters who are gifted. A broad approach to career awareness for gifted students should address the following issues:

» self-awareness (i.e., understanding one's personal values, interests, personality, and skills);
» understanding present and future career options;
» understanding how high school courses, college majors, and advanced degrees relate to careers;
» understanding that multiple interests can be combined into a career;
» participating in internships, mentorships, and other hands-on experiences; and
» understanding that some interests are associated with specific careers and some interests become leisure activities. Gifted adults are unlikely to find self-fulfillment through work alone.

Resources and Assessment Tools for Career Exploration

Aptitude tests, interest inventories, other standardized instruments, and a variety of additional resources are used by school systems, counselors, and teachers to help students learn about themselves and set short- and long-term educational and career goals. These instruments are useful because they provide a great deal of information in a minimal amount of time. Some instruments provide information at a relatively low cost. However, most aptitude tests and interest inventories must be used with caution for the following reasons:

» Some tests designed for the general public are inappropriate for gifted students, who tend to score in the 98th to 99th percentiles in all areas, because the ceiling is too low. Many gifted students score in the uppermost deciles in all scales, demonstrating a high, flat profile. These students doubt the usefulness of the tests.

» Most aptitude tests cannot discriminate among high levels of performance; thus, they do not reflect the relative strengths and weaknesses of gifted students.

A variety of instruments may be useful for adults who wish to provide gifted students with information about themselves to use in short- and long-term planning. This includes tools for values clarification and appropriate inventories that assess interests, personal needs, and learning styles. Values clarification encourages students to understand themselves better and to develop belief systems and behavior codes that they can later use as a foundation for some of the most important decisions of their lives. Interest inventories are designed to help students understand themselves, their possible career directions, and the educational preparation necessary for various career alternatives. Some inventories do not give gifted students sufficient information about careers that have existed for only a few years; however, combined with values clarification, decision-making skills, and appropriate group and individual guidance counseling, these instruments can be helpful. Personal needs assessments help students understand the ways in which their personality characteristics integrate with careers. Learning style inventories help students understand the way they prefer to learn.

The following instruments are appropriate for gifted students. Many of them are available in a computerized version.

» **The Harrington-O'Shea Career Decision-Making System—Revised**, available from Pearson Assessments (https://www.pearsonassessments.com/ OR http://careercompetencies.org/). The design of this tool makes it easy to administer, and it provides most students with an adequate interpretation of their preferences. However, it does not distinguish among some science clusters. For example, the student whose primary interest is physical science may not produce scores indicating science as a preferred career category, if he or she rejects

87

life science activities. The Career Decision-Making System has a variety of levels in English and Spanish.

» **The Career Occupational Preference System (COPS)**, published by Educational & Industrial Testing Service (http://www.edits.net/products/copsystem.html). COPS, for grades 6 through 12, matches interests with certain career clusters. Because distinctions are made between different science clusters—for example, physical science, life science, and mathematical science—this test has been used successfully with gifted students.

» **Self-Directed Search** (**SDS**; http://www.self-directed-search.com/) is a career interest test that asks questions about your aspirations, activities, skills, and interests in different jobs. From the responses, the SDS produces your personal three-letter Summary Code, which you can use to find occupations and fields of study that match well with your personality. Holland (1962) developed his model by analyzing responses from National Merit finalists, which suggests that it should be relevant for use with gifted individuals. Gifted adolescents often find the Holland theory of vocational choice helpful because it generates a three-letter "Holland Code," based on inclusion in the following groups: (1) realistic type, which likes to work with things (e.g., tools, objects, machines, or animals); (2) investigative type, which tends to be curious, studious, and independent, and will be successful in any area in which creative problem defining or problem solving is valued; (3) artistic type, which is creative, free-wheeling, and tends to dislike routine; (4) social type, which prefers activities in which the primary focus is on helping other people; (5) enterprising type, which likes activities that permit leading or influencing other people; and (6) conventional type, which likes activities that permit organization of information in a clear and orderly way. The most successful people in fields associated with this type are outgoing, energetic, persistent people who are committed to an idea.

Students can use this tool by imagining they are at a party and people from each of the above six groups are gathered in separate locations in a room. Which group are you most attracted to? Select three groups this way and write down the first letter of each of the three groups you would prefer to spend time with. That will give you your own 3-letter code. Now, go online to the University of Missouri Career Center website (http://career. missouri.edu/index.php/career-interest-game) and match your codes with their job possibilities by running your mouse over each group heading.

This exercise will give students a general idea of the career possibilities to think about. The exercise can also be played online at the SDS website (http://www.self-directed-search.com). They will give you feedback for a small fee.

Software

Technological advancement has added a new dimension to career counseling—computer-based career information and guidance systems. Interviews indicate that computer-based career information and guidance systems are being used successfully with gifted students, including the DISCOVER and SIGI software programs.

DISCOVER, available from the American College Testing Program (ACT; http://www.act.org/discover), was developed as a systematic career guidance program to assist in career development activities at the secondary school level. The package includes values and decision-making education, relating and exploring occupations, and career exploration and planning.

SIGI3 (System of Interactive Guidance and Information; http://www.sigi3.org), originally published by Educational Testing Service (ETS), is based on the assumption that a person's values are the overriding factor in his or her career choice. The computer system weighs the relative strengths of 10 values (including income, level of independence, helping others, security, fields of interest, and leadership) and tests the user by considering combinations of hypothetical jobs, each of which stresses one particular value. When values conflict, the computer warns the user of the discrepancy and asks the user to reconsider. For example, if a student says, "I want to help people" and "earn $100,000 a year," the program recognizes a conflict in goals and provides alternatives (http://www.sigi3.org/What-SIGI3-Does.html).

In summary, online tools to help students explore career options are expanding. In late 2013, ACT launched ACT Profile (https://www.actprofile.org), designed for high school students to use with their counselors to help in the college-search process. The site includes interest inventories, a section for students to search colleges based on their personal criteria, such as size and location, and a place for students to upload their work and establish an electronic portfolio. The College Board also has an online resource, BigFuture (https://bigfuture.collegeboard.org/), to help students plan, research, and pay for college. To help students explore college costs, the U.S. Department of Education's College Affordability and Transparency Center (http://collegecost. ed.gov/catc/) can help students comparison shop (Adams, 2013).

What Parents Can Do

If your school has a career center, volunteer. If possible, set up a program that matches students with adults in careers. However, speakers should be carefully chosen for their ability to relate to adolescents. Students are generally interested in any or all of the following:

» the nature of the person's work;
» prior work experiences leading to the person's current position;
» how the person became interested in the work;
» the advantages and disadvantages, positive and negative aspects of the work;
» a typical workday;

» formal educational preparation;
» college courses the person found most valuable;
» college courses the person wishes he or she had taken;
» the long-range job opportunities in the person's field; and
» the current and potential salary range.

Talk about your work—its positive and negative aspects, its advantages and disadvantages, and future opportunities in the field. If possible, take your adolescent where you work and show him or her what you do. In addition, ask open-ended questions when your student mentions careers. (Avoid statements that inadvertently transmit expectations.) Encourage your child to explore in depth as many careers as possible, and encourage community involvement, particularly volunteer activities. Overall, keep in mind that many people change careers several times during their work life.

What Teachers Can Do

Teachers, you should assist students in career planning in the following ways:

» Discuss teaching and specific fields of teaching with students—including the educational requirements, advantages and disadvantages, and future opportunities.
» Encourage students to read biographies and other material about people who work in education.
» Encourage girls to explore mathematical and scientific fields.
» Encourage boys to explore the humanities and/or a liberal arts college, especially if they plan to pursue a specialized mathematical or scientific field.
» Discuss ways that your discipline is related to different careers.
» Provide opportunities for students to write critically and speak effectively about the way their careers might relate to the future.

What Counselors Can Do

Career planning is most effective when designed as a coherent 4-year program in which, by the end of 11th grade, gifted students can ask and begin to answer the following questions:

» How is school related to my personal career goals?
» How do vocational assessments and inventories relate to my goals?
» What specific steps can I take to explore and investigate fields that appear to be appropriate for me?
» What type of research will give me answers to questions I ask?
» How can I get an apprenticeship, internship, or mentor?
» What types of work activities do I prefer?
» What types of work situations do I like?
» What careers do I want to avoid? Why?

4 Learning About Colleges
What Do They Have That I Want?

There are more than 3,500 colleges in the United States. Some are more selective than others. Some are "name brand" colleges, but some of the nation's best colleges are not well-known. Most people find a college where they are happy. If you have done some college planning homework, you know which classes you like the most and the type of activities you enjoy. You have used some of the tools and resources in Chapter 3 and have at least thought about your strengths and how to match strengths with potential college majors. The price of your degree increases incrementally every year, so you owe it to yourself to make the most of the opportunity to attend college. Avoiding the common pitfalls (Figure 5) is part of that.

A word about academic success. There is a huge difference between high school and college, particularly the level of independence and personal freedom. High school is mandatory and free; college is voluntary and expensive. In high school, students do not have complete control over the way they spend their time. In college, they are free to set their own schedules. High school teachers may approach the student who is having academic problems. College faculty members are less likely to approach students, although they are likely to be helpful and friendly when students seek assistance. Some students never needed to study

"I'm applying to college X because all my friends are/are not going there."

"There's only one college that's right for me."

"All colleges are the same, so why bother with all this work?"

"I'm going to college X because my father/mother/sister/brother went there (or wants me to go there)."

"College X is too expensive for me."

"I'm not applying there because I'll be rejected." (This does not mean you should avoid applying to one "long-shot" school.)

"If the one college I want doesn't want me, I'll be unhappy for the next 4 years."

Figure 5. Common pitfalls for students.

during high school. College is probably the end of that. Successful college students study for several hours outside of class for each hour spent in class. Students who disliked high school because of its structure may be much happier in college. Students who are happier when a structure is imposed may have a bumpy transitional path during their freshman year.

MOOCs Versus In-class Learning

Online courses called MOOCs, or *massive open online courses,* provide a solution for some students who prefer online learning. MOOCs are videotaped lectures translated by grad students versed in online education. According to The *New York Times* (Pappano, 2012), edX, the nonprofit start–up from Harvard and the Massachusetts Institute of Technology, has 370,000 students in its first official courses. Coursera, another start–up, has reached more than 1.7 million.

1. Gathering information
2. Planning and choosing
3. Making two visits
4. Applying
5. Interviewing and writing an essay
6. Applying for financial aid
7. Making acceptance decisions

Figure 6. Seven steps of the college planning process.

This chapter describes the process of learning about colleges (see Figure 6 for the seven steps of the process).

STEP 1: GATHERING INFORMATION

Step 1 of the college search process involves collecting general information by visiting websites, reading guidebooks and using multimedia resources, talking with people (asking questions), and visiting colleges. Websites provide databases of colleges such as the College Board, Peterson's, and others listed in Appendix B. Depending on the site, you may be able to type in the geographical area, size, setting, major(s), and other characteristics that interest you. The database then produces a list of colleges that match your preferences. These comparative sites are a great way to generate a long list of colleges to research further. You might find colleges you haven't even thought of. Some comparative sites only include the colleges that pay for the privilege of being listed, so you could miss some good options if you rely on only one site. You'll find that some comparative sites have more up-to-date information than others about individual colleges. For the most up-to-date information, it's best to check the colleges' websites directly.

What Students Can Do to Learn About Colleges

You know a lot about yourself, your strengths and weaknesses, and your choices. You can do the following to learn about colleges and college offerings:

» Look at the college information available in your counselor's office and school and public libraries.
» Become familiar with different types of college guides and multimedia resources.
» Ask questions. Talk to college students, graduates, and college representatives.
» Visit a wide range of colleges.

College Guidebooks and Multimedia Resources

There are two types of college guides: *objective reference guides* that provide information from a database, such as number of students or average SATs, and *subjective guides* that provide information based on opinion, such as "10 hottest schools."

Objective Guides. Objective guides provide categorical and statistical data on every 2- and/or 4-year college and university in the United States, Canada, and other countries. They list colleges and universities alphabetically or by state; most also list the telephone number for the Office of Admissions. The following guides offer data-based information. Because they are updated every year, the ISBN numbers and years have not been listed for these resources; however, a current copy of each can easily be found at your local library or bookstore or an online bookseller. Watch out for publication dates. Some books are not published annually. Many books come with CDs and most offer comprehensive online information.

» Barron's Online College Search Engine (http://www. barronspac.com)
» College Board BigFuture (https://bigfuture.collegeboard. org/)
» *Fiske Guide to Colleges 2014* (http://www.fiskeguide.com)

» *Peterson's Four-Year Colleges* (http://www.petersons. com/college-search.aspx)
» *The Princeton Review* and The Princeton Review Blog (http://in.princetonreview.com/)

In addition, you may want to check out the Princeton Review's *The Best 378 Colleges, 2014 Edition* (Princeton Review, 2013).

Objective guides provide data-based college profiles that are written by the colleges and, hence, may be designed to cast each college in a favorable light. However, this fact does not negate their usefulness. Objective college guides contain similar information but differ in several ways:

» Some objective guides have specific orientations; for example, a section on careers. The section may be useful, but it may not be appropriate for every gifted student.
» Some objective guides are more thorough than others in breadth, depth, and scope of coverage.
» Some objective guides include worksheets that allow students to map the college selection process; this is particularly useful for some students.
» Some objective guides are revised annually and contain up-to-date information on the cost of tuition, room, and board.
» A companion index of majors accompanies some objective guides. This index provides information for students who know what they want to study, but not where to study it. The index is particularly helpful to students who want to combine academic majors (e.g., physics and philosophy) or major in an area that is relatively uncommon (e.g., a specialized microbiological science).

The statistical information provided by objective guides can be used in different ways. For example, most college profiles list the number of undergraduate students enrolled. When you visit a college, investigate the relationship between college size and the size of an average freshman class. You may find that some classes are gigantic, but the college offers supplemental freshman seminars. The size of the student body will affect your opportunities and experiences, including the range of academic majors offered and extracurricular possibilities. When considering size, look beyond the raw number of students who attend the school to the size of the department that interests you. Is the faculty in this department accessible to the students?

Guides also list admissions standards, including the school's basis for selection and the average SAT and/or ACT scores of entering freshmen. The average scores are not adjusted to reflect students who leave the school prior to graduation. You can use the graphic breakdown of each institution's SAT/ACT scores to determine how comfortable you will be academically. Based on this information, if your scores fall in the top or middle of the range, you will probably be comfortable at this school. The other way to see how you compare is to look at the SAT or ACT scores of the latest graduating class in your high school. Find students who were admitted to the colleges you are looking at. Compare your scores. Of course this method doesn't take into account unpredictability—that the scores earned by your class could be much higher than previous classes.

Subjective Guides. Subjective guides are similar to objective guides, but limit the colleges discussed to specific groups, or focus on specific topics. Unlike many objective guides, these books are updated often, but not necessarily every year.

» *Admission Matters: What Students and Parents Need to Know About Getting into College,* 3rd ed. (2013) by Sally P. Springer, Jon Reider, and Joyce Vining Morgan

» *U.S. News Best Colleges 2014* by U.S. News & World Report

» *The Insider's Guide to the Colleges, 2014: Students on Campus Tell You What You Really Want to Know* by the Yale Daily News Staff

» *America's Best Colleges for B Students: A College Guide for Students Without Straight A's* (2013) by Tamra B. Orr

» *College Bound: Proven Ways to Plan and Prepare for Getting Into the College of Your Dreams* (2013) by Christine M. Hand-Gonzales, Ed.D.

Objective and subjective guides are used differently. In effect, subjective guides supplement objective guides. Keep in mind the following:

» Some subjective guides may not specify criteria used to rank colleges. Descriptions may in fact be one person's biased opinion, formulated during a brief, one-time visit.

» Some subjective guides rank academic departments in selected colleges; however, they may not state the criteria they have used to do so. The information may be valuable when verified during a college visit, particularly if you arrange an interview with a faculty member.

» Many college rankings change from year to year. For example, a college that was ranked No. 2 one year could drop to No. 8 the next year, or a school that was in the second tier could jump up to a top-20 category. The school might not have changed; however, the formula used for ranking colleges might have been revised. If two different magazines rank colleges differently (e.g., one uses the number of acceptances divided by the number of applications, and the other uses the yield, or the number of enrollments divided by the number of acceptances), the two different methods will produce different rankings.

» Some subjective guides only discuss student life or a specific aspect of campus lifestyle, so make sure you use a more comprehensive guide, as well.

Objective guides may be pallid, but they are often more useful than colorful subjective guides. For example, one guide may note that a school's graduate students do not teach undergraduate courses, while another may state that the university population is divided into several social cliques. Anecdotal information may be entertaining, but it also may be biased or misleading. If you want to find out how many students in a particular school graduate with a business degree (statistical information), consult an objective guide. If you want to find out about the social scene at a particular school, consult a responsible subjective guide, preferably one that collects information through questionnaires distributed to enrolled college students. Bear in mind that the social scene at every college varies from year to year and that some descriptions have been written by students who graduated prior to the book's publication date. If you are using an online guide, make sure it's the most recent version.

Newspapers such as *The New York Times* have useful blogs about college planning (http://thechoice.blogs.nytimes.com). The College Board also has a blog called BigFuture, which includes a college search tool as well as a scholarship search tool and a customizable action plan for students about to embark on journeys through the college admissions process (https://bigfuture.collegeboard.org/find-colleges/college-101/types-of-colleges-the-basics).

Additional Resources

The first information students receive from colleges usually arrives by e-mail or postal mail. Students who have taken the PSAT may feel bombarded with information. Familiarize yourself with the differences between degree-granting colleges, technical schools, and public or private universities so you can begin some sort of filing system—even if the system consists of empty shoe boxes.

Websites, view books, and glossy brochures are designed to promote the college's physical appearance and campus facilities. Larger schools with many resources may emphasize technological equipment or champion sports teams. Smaller schools with fewer resources might emphasize a homey atmosphere. These publications provide superficial information that should be confirmed during a campus visit.

College websites, often a student's first point of contact with a college, may take students on a narrated, picturesque visit, presenting an idyllic physical setting with students studying under a tree on a lovely spring day. Keep in mind that this idyllic scene may occur for a short period each year.

To make the most of a college's website, try these strategies.

» Look at the home pages of individual faculty members in majors that interest you—some post detailed syllabuses of their classes, descriptions of their research interests, and e-mail addresses. If you have a specific question or two about a major, try sending a faculty member a short, polite e-mail introducing yourself and asking your questions (but don't ask anything you can find out in the catalog or on the website).

» Read the pages for prospective students thoroughly. They will give you basic information about the college, as well as some sense of the mission and priorities of the college.

» Visit the home pages of student organizations and check out the various clubs and groups.

» Find the alumni association pages—what are alumni of the college doing now? What is the college doing for its alumni?

Many high school career centers or libraries provide commercial computerized databases that are advertised and purchased by school systems. Data Lists (http://www.data-lists.com) is one example and is downloadable for a fee. Similar databases are provided to school systems by the major college guides such as College Board and Princeton Review. The software is easy to use and offers fast access to information. The more sophisticated programs are interactive, menu-driven, and offer a college selection service, financial aid information, and career exploration. They also offer a "why not?" option that tells users why certain colleges or career choices were not included. The scholarship search allows users to match individual characteristics, such as ethnic and multicultural backgrounds or special talents, with sources of aid, such as national and state grants and public and private scholarships.

Every college and university publishes a *catalog* describing the institution and the courses it offers. Some colleges charge a fee for the catalog unless you download it from their website. College catalogs can help you assess a school's distribution requirements, the kinds of courses taught, and the sizes of various academic departments. This will help you decide whether or not a particular college will meet your academic and career needs. Bear in mind that although one particular course may sound interesting, that course may not be taught each semester and may even be dropped by the time you enroll. If you are interested in specific courses, ask about them when you visit a campus. You can request information from colleges using the sample request letter in Figure 7.

Take advantage of opportunities to obtain different types of information by asking questions of college representatives, college students, teachers, and others who can provide firsthand knowledge. If you know what you want to study, research reputations of academic departments by talking to people in the fields that interest you. Consider, compare, and evaluate information you receive. If you're undecided, relax and pick an academically balanced institution that offers a range of majors and programs. Most colleges offer counseling to help you find a focus.

College representatives who represent their schools at college fairs can answer the following questions:

> » What makes your college different from all other colleges?
> » How does the college evaluate applicants?
> » How does the school evaluate SAT or ACT scores?
> » Does the college require students to take specific courses or enroll in courses to fulfill certain requirements (i.e., distribution requirements/core curriculum)?
> » Do students have the same adviser every year?

Director of Admissions
College of Your Choice
Address

To Whom It May Concern:
    I am a student at _____ High School in (city and state). I plan to graduate in (month) of 20____. Please send me a copy of your latest college catalog and an application form. I also would like to receive forms for all types of financial aid. I am considering majoring in _____ , am also interested in _____ , and would appreciate any information about these concentrations.
    Thank you very much for your assistance. I look forward to hearing from you soon.

Sincerely,
Your Name

Figure 7. Sample request for written information.

» What procedures exist for orientation, advising, and registration? Can I register for classes by computer?
» How does the college assist students with career planning?
» Is the admissions process "need blind"? Are merit-based scholarships available?

College students can answer the following questions:
» What do you like and dislike about the location?
» Why did you select that college?
» What do you wish you had known before selecting this school?
» What is campus life like? What are the "hot topics"?
» When you started college, what differences did you notice between high school and college?
» What is your average day like?

» How do you live? What kind of living arrangements does the college offer, and is housing guaranteed to anyone who wants to live on campus? What are the advantages and disadvantages of living on and off campus?

» Who teaches most of your classes? Professors or graduate students? Are some classes offered online for credit?

» Where do students study? Are the dorms quiet enough to study in your room?

» What kinds of relationships exist between students and faculty, and between the college and the town or city where it is located?

» What provisions are made for students' physical and mental health, safety, and security?

» Does the school help you plan a career? If so, how?

When you gather information, be sure to consider the different types of colleges and universities. You will find more information by searching the "Carnegie Classifications of Institutions of Higher Education" on Wikipedia. You can see that Carnegie categorized some schools by the highest level degree awarded. A more common way to categorize is the following:

» *Small liberal arts colleges*: Likely to have smaller classes and no graduate students; may not have the programs of study that interest you.

» *Large private universities*: Often highly selective, with a wide range of programs. A small, but growing, trend at larger universities offers students the best of both worlds: residential colleges, a long-held tradition at some Ivy League schools, provide students with smaller communities within large universities.

» *State universities:* These often have open admission and must accept applicants from their state until a cut-off date.

» *Women's colleges*: Most are now coeducational, but the majority of their students are women. Their faculty also is made up primarily of women. Many prominent women claim a women's college as their alma mater.

» *Technical universities*: May emphasize computer science, math, and science. The word *technical* is part of their name (e.g., California Institute of Technology [Cal Tech] or Virginia Polytechnic Institute and State University [Virginia Tech]).

» *Comprehensive mid-size schools*: A middle ground, larger than small liberal arts schools, but smaller than private universities or state schools. Usually, these schools do not have graduate students or teaching assistants.

» *Doctorate-granting research universities*: Often have renowned faculty who are known for their cutting-edge research and publications. However, they may not teach undergraduate students. If you want to attend a top research university to learn from renowned faculty, find out if these faculty members teach classes or focus solely on research and publishing.

In addition to finding out what type of college you're applying to, you should also look for information about its admissions options. Different colleges and universities have different types of admissions options, including early decision (ED), early action (EA), and single-choice early action (SCEA).

Early decision (ED) is the application process in which students make a commitment to a first-choice institution where, if admitted, they definitely will enroll. *Early action* (EA) is the application process in which students submit an application to an institution of preference and receive a decision well in advance of the institution's regular response rate. *Single-choice early action* (SCEA), also referred to as nonbinding early decision, can best be described as a midpoint between early decision and early action (NACAC, 2001, 2004b). Similar to ED, if a student applies to an SCEA college, the student is prohibited from applying either ED or EA to other colleges, but may apply regular admission anywhere else. Unlike ED and similar to EA, students are not bound to attend the SCEA college if they are accepted.

Whether any of these policies offers the student an advantage depends on the year. Some years a college will offer the early decision admission option to quite a few applicants, and other years they do not offer early admission to any applicants. The colleges are inconsistent on these admissions policies, so it's best to ask. Some colleges have rigid formulas for Early Decision (ED) candidates. Does applying as an Early Decision candidate increase your chance of admission? There are conflicting theories on that. Some argue that well-qualified ED applicants have a slight edge over their regular admission candidates because the pool is smaller and the school knows that it is the applicant's first choice. Others believe that the competition is stronger because the field is smaller and therefore they have a better chance in the regular pool. It is never wise to become part of a group of frenzied students, particularly if a final list of college choices has not been assembled and a final choice is not really final. If ED is simply an admission strategy, wait. If you need financial assistance, wait.

Early Action (EA) is for students who want to test the waters, without a commitment. Some colleges use their EA program as a barometer for scholarship competition. Remember if a student applicant is accepted under ED, all EA applications must be withdrawn. If you are denied early, you are done with that college. You cannot reapply in the regular round or ED II. They have decided that they know enough about you to make a final decision. Some colleges have admissions rates two or three higher for ED applicants compared with regular decision applicants and they fill from one-third to almost half of their freshman classes from the early pool. Because colleges vary widely, read school websites, and if in doubt, ask an admissions officer. Some schools have been openly telling legacy applicants that their legacy hook will count only if they apply early, reinforcing the idea of early decision as a strategy (Springer, Reider, & Morgan, 2013).

Organizing Information

If you have taken the PSATs, SATs, ACTs, or any other standardized test, you may receive information from colleges sometime in the near future. The volume and variety of information you receive can be confusing if you do not organize it in some way. In general, your life will be calmer if you figure out a system. Any method will do, even if it seems haphazard. Your particular method is not important, as long as you are organized, your system is consistent, and you understand what you are doing. For example, you can construct a chart, set up a color-coded file, or develop a computer database. You can start with three cartons, labeled yes, no way, and maybe.

STEP 2: PLANNING AND CHOOSING

During 11th grade or the summer before 12th grade, college-bound adolescents should have enough information to be able to plan and choose; that is, develop a list of 10 to 20 colleges based on personal criteria—what you know about yourself, your skills, and interests. (If you want to combine the last year of high school with one year of college, this process will need to be accelerated by at least a year.) Students, be sure the list includes schools where you *might* be accepted, schools where you will *probably* be accepted, and schools where you *know* you will be accepted. Your decision should be based on what you know about yourself and your values, interests, personal needs, and goals; what you learn about colleges and college offerings; and an understanding of how colleges evaluate applicants. This is not an easy task, in part because your interests, needs, and goals may change and in part because college admission standards change each year. Keep in mind that there are about 100 selective schools, schools that may reject more applications than they accept. That leaves more than 3,500 that can go on your list of "definites."

Once you have a preliminary list of colleges that interest you, the Internet can be helpful in researching each college further. The primary ways to research colleges online are through the individual college websites and through e-mail contact. Once you get to the school's website, plan on spending some time investigating. You can find all of the basics—selectivity, size, majors, setting, etc.—in addition to some clues as to what everyday life on campus is like. When you start looking at college websites, you will find two types of information: the official information you can get from the admissions office and the college catalog, and the unofficial information you get when you read the student newspaper or contact current students. Both are valuable. Keep in mind that marketing firms have developed the official pages in order to sell you something—the school.

At this point in the college planning process, you need a way of organizing the information you have gathered so you can make some choices. Rank ordering the criteria that are important to you is a way to get started. Figure 8 will help you look at each school using the same criteria. If a criterion is not important, skip it and go on to the next.

Good decisions require good decision-making skills and good information. Two categories of good information are required:

> » *Information about yourself.* Think about your interests and the experiences you have had that you really enjoyed. Let your imagination run wild and picture yourself at work. What kinds of people do you like to spend time with? Information about yourself will permit you to list the characteristics you want in a college. These should include some of the following: the college's location, type, size, social life, academic environment, campus environment, religious affiliation, student activities, programs offered, special programs, caliber of students, cost, athletics, financial aid, housing, school calendar, and other factors.

> » *Information about the world of choices.* This should include academic experiences and interests. The stronger your

Here are some criteria you may want to use when selecting a range of colleges. First, go through the list to determine which criteria are important to you. (Your choices might change as you learn more about schools.) Then, as you investigate colleges, fill in the names of several in the top row. Rate each characteristic on a scale of 1 to 5, based on its importance to you. Then, use your rankings to help you make a decision about which colleges you'd like to apply to.

When you select colleges, bear in mind that your list should include at least one safety school, one long shot, and several schools whose selection criteria match your qualifications.

School Name:			
Characteristics	**Scale 1–5 (Poor to Excellent)**		
Size			
Location			
Cost			
Type			
Social Life			
Academic Atmosphere			
Campus Environment			
Religious Affiliation			
Student Activities			
Programs Offered			
Special Programs			
Campus Lifestyle			
Caliber of Students			
Athletics			
Financial Aid			
Housing			
Faculty			
Calendar			
Prestige			

Figure 8. Determining criteria.

School Name:			
Characteristics	Scale 1–5 (Poor to Excellent)		
Special Services			
Distribution			
Requirements			
Selectivity			
Other			

Figure 8. Continued.

academic preparation, the broader your range of options. Make a rank-ordered list of your extracurricular experiences and interests. Eventually, your choices will reflect your personal values, attitudes, aptitudes, interests, goals, and finances. Information about your choices comes from several sources, including your counselor, college fairs, the Internet, and various other media-related resources. Start with your guidance office. Become familiar with the college guides, multimedia resources, and videotapes in your counselor's office. Collect literature from college fairs. Obtain literature from your top 15 to 20 choices.

Planning and choosing involves analyzing and evaluating information you have obtained from people, written material, and websites. Visiting a school is the primary way to confirm what you have discovered and separate fact from fiction. By the middle of 12th grade, you should narrow your list to five or six colleges by evaluating information about college offerings and the method used by colleges to select a freshman class. (If you are going to apply for early decision, this process will have to take place well before the middle of 12th grade.) The final list should reflect (a) personal values, interests, and needs; (b) the variety and range of available college opportunities; and (c) realistic constraints, such as cost and distance.

At this point, selectivity of the schools on the list should also be considered, because you are looking for a match between your needs and school offerings. Selectivity means the number of students accepted compared to the number who applied. As the number of applications increases, its admission rate decreases. A selective school is generally thought of as one that accepts less than half of its applicants. If you choose a highly selective school, you must prepare yourself for rigorous academics. Keep in mind what we said above: except for highly selective "Ivy" schools, which in some years accept less than 10%, and moderately selective schools that accept less than 20% of applicants, the rest of the pool of schools admits more than 50% of its applicants. Those numbers change when graduating high school seniors decide which school to actually attend. The yield, that is, the number of students who actually enroll, may be higher or lower. The popular perception fueled by media, guidebooks, and the colleges themselves is much more narrow or selective. It is true that many freshmen attend colleges that are their third or fourth choice, but from another perspective, there is a school for everyone who is willing to work hard. Every year the National Association for College Admission Counseling posts a list on its website of more than 200 colleges still seeking applicants (Springer et al., 2013).

To form a list of colleges that will be a good match for your interests and needs, you should know how colleges evaluate applicants so that you can compare your credentials with those of enrolled students.

> » *Academic performance.* Every college first looks at a student's academic performance—the courses you took and the grades you earned in those courses. Many advanced courses are offered in sequence, so they will look first at 11th and 12th grade, and then look to see if there is an upward trend in the challenge level of the courses and the grades you earned. Every year of high school is important.

» *Standardized test scores.* Standardized tests (PSATs, SATs, ACTs, and SAT Subject Tests) are the only objective way a college can compare you to a student in some other part of the country. Most colleges want to know how successful you will be if you attend their college, and even if they don't request or use your scores, a low score on your transcript will get their attention and raise some questions.

» *Extracurricular activities.* After reviewing your academic performance and scores, admissions officers next look at your extracurricular activities and the way you spend your time when you are not in school. Colleges look for depth, commitment, initiative, and leadership, not for an exhaustive list.

» *Supporting material.* When highly selective colleges decide between two students who are on par academically, the creative presentation of extracurricular activities, the quality of recommendations, the essay or personal statement, the interview, and other written material can tip the balance in your favor.

Tips for Parents

As your family begins to talk about colleges, here are some things to watch for. Don't let your teen make these common college planning mistakes when choosing a list of colleges.

» Attempting to change themselves to fit to the college. A student may create five different "selves" to present to five different colleges. These students need assistance in knowing and presenting their true best selves as accurately as possible. This requires some planning and record-keeping.

» Abandoning common sense in investigating colleges. A college does not want to be evaluated solely on the basis of its students' SAT or ACT scores any more than you want to be evaluated solely on the basis of your SAT or ACT scores.

» Letting themselves be excessively influenced by college guidebooks and videos. These materials range in value, with some containing misleading information and others providing up-to-date, accurate information. Also, subjective books that evaluate colleges are often judgmental and may not state the criteria used for ranking schools.

» Spending too much time trying to gain a competitive edge in the process. Some students take the ACTs or SATs repeatedly or spend many hours thinking about a part of the process that is less important than grades or standardized tests.

» Letting the results of the college admission process affect a student's self-esteem. This is important!

Parents, when your student is comfortable with a self-evaluation process and begins to view himself in terms of his values, interests, skills, and personal needs rather than in terms of his strengths and weaknesses, he is prepared to begin the exploration of college offerings. The better the self-knowledge the student has, the better the student will be able to match his or her goals, expectations, and requirements with those of a college. This matching process carries several cautionary notes.

Educators and counselors interviewed for this book indicated that gifted students become anxious about applying to college as early as seventh grade, although they may not know basic college planning facts, such as what courses will appear on a high school transcript. They need reassurance; for example, remind them that college decisions do not have to be made prior to 11th or 12th grade. However, reassurance unaccompanied by information and a coherent plan is rarely sufficient for gifted students.

Gifted students need to understand that college planning is part of a lengthy career planning process; it need not be an isolated event that begins and ends mysteriously or arbitrarily.

Learning about colleges is one part of a broad-based approach to planning for college, designing career goals, and, ultimately, leading a personally satisfying life.

During their latter years of high school, some gifted students seem to perfect the art of procrastination. Multipotential students may not be ready to select priorities; they may be academically successful in all courses and unable to focus. Students sensitive to the pressure of expectations may develop a case of advanced paralysis each time someone asks, "Where do you want to go to college?" Both groups swing from one unrealistic extreme to another. They decide on a college or career one day, and the next day they reject that choice and wonder how they will ever decide. These students may procrastinate until the 11th hour. Although this is common, parents become impatient as they realize the complexity of the application process and how little it resembles their own experiences. Parents may urge students to make a decision based on cost or apply to colleges previously attended by family members, but if the match is to be a good one, the student should be the primary matchmaker.

The increasing number and variety of books on how to get accepted by the college of your choice adds to everyone's anxiety. Students say these books are helpful because they learn how to market themselves. However, many books inadvertently reinforce the idea that college planning begins with November SATs or ACTs and ends with letters of acceptance from the student's chosen schools.

College and career planning may be particularly difficult for some gifted students. However, it can be a growth-promoting experience for all participants when the ultimate goal, student decisions based on realistic criteria that result in a satisfying life, is kept at the forefront of all decision-making activity.

STEP 3: VISITING COLLEGES

Applying to a college you haven't seen is like buying shoes by mail; it's simply impossible to know if you'll be comfortable.
—Dean of Admissions, small public university

Visiting colleges is Step 3 in your college search. You may have gathered a lot of information (Step 1) by reading the guides and asking questions. You may have started planning and choosing (Step 2) by comparing your scores to the scores of admitted students in some schools, or analyzing other types of information, such as the difference between selective and highly selective schools. Schools are like people. They are quite different in values, culture, and beliefs. They have different personalities, and it's difficult to sense the differences without walking through the campus and talking to students. Visiting colleges is the only way to acquire firsthand information and test your conclusions, and it is the only justifiable way to make final college selection decisions. Most experts recommend that students visit no earlier than during the second semester of junior year. The reason is that students are not quite ready to focus. It takes time to reflect, and students go through so many changes during high school. The "self" they know in 10th grade may not be the same "self" they know a year later. In addition, teens are so busy during junior year they have a difficult time remembering what they saw a year before.

So what does a visit offer that students can't get from the Internet or friends? A visit offers an opportunity to look beneath the ivy and examine the bricks. If a campus visit isn't possible before you have to narrow your list of applications, you can always visit before you have to make a final choice.

Campus visits are most effective when conducted in two stages. Plan to collect different types of information during each stage. Timing depends on a number of things, including your schedule and your family's schedule. You should begin to visit campuses during your junior year in high school. If you want to consider applying for early decision, you must start earlier and combine the following steps.

Stage One Visits

You should plan to visit approximately eight to 12 colleges that look interesting and to which you think you might apply. Part of this tour is to compare colleges and universities and their differences. A college tour will be easier if the colleges you want to see are located in one state or adjoining states. A family-team approach works best for this type of "grand tour." If you have younger siblings, take them along, because they might notice things that you do not see, and the trip will help familiarize them with college campuses. Make the first college trip fun! Be sure to go online for a campus map for each school you plan to visit. Call each admissions office in advance and ask some of the following questions:

>> Where is the nearest place to stay overnight?
>> Are there any other colleges nearby?
>> Will we be able to park on campus?
>> What time are guided tours and group information sessions? How long do they last?
>> Are students enrolled in the regular fall or spring semester currently taking classes on your campus?
>> Are any campus activities planned for the day we plan to visit?
>> Does the school offer on-campus interviews? If I want a personal interview with the dean of admissions or a representative, can you make suggestions about timing?

During the campus visit, you and your family should plan to accomplish the following:

>> Take a guided tour.
>> Visit several campus buildings.
>> Eat in the dining halls.

» Read the student newspaper and bulletin boards.
» Ask questions of the admissions office, students, and faculty.
» Tour the surrounding area. Ask questions about the weather, shopping, and the community.
» Take good notes during each visit; record your impressions as soon as possible. Pick up an application and other information.

If the visit includes a personal interview, write a prompt thank-you note to the interviewer. The personal note will reinforce the interviewer's memory of you and can be especially helpful if you are interviewed on a day when the admissions officer has seen many applicants.

If a trip is well planned and you take good notes, you will gather a lot of informal information in a short time. A word of caution: If an initial visit is planned for summer, the students on campus may not be typical of the student body present during the regular term. The goal of the first visit, however, is to collect general information and answer the question, "Do I think I would be happy here?" You may require a second visit to secure specific information, present your student credentials to the college, and ask, "What are my chances for admission to this school in my major?"

Following the first visits, sift through the information collected, talk with your parents and counselor, and narrow the list of possibilities. You should now be able to prepare a rank-ordered list of four to six colleges where you will probably be comfortable. If this is not possible, then additional campus visits or a different approach to analyzing the information gathered is necessary. It's better not to make a final decision on the basis of the first visit, especially if you did not stay in a dormitory. Some colleges will gauge your interest by the number of times you have contacted a school. If you visit twice, call for an interview, and ask good questions, a school will assume that you have a deeper interest than the student who just "drops in" for a visit.

Stage Two Visits

The second visit helps you reach final decisions. Here, timing may be more important than for the first visit. A stage two visit during late winter or early spring helps both you and the colleges. Between January (the date when most student applications must reach a college) and April (the month when colleges traditionally send out acceptance letters), colleges have the most information about their pool of applicants, available scholarship money, and other factors. They may be able to provide you with concrete information that will help you reach a final decision. Therefore, after completing the application process, you should try to revisit the campuses that interest you for at least 1 to 2 days each, preferably while classes are in session. Use the questions in this guide and the information you have gathered to develop a list of key questions to ask during this second visit.

Guidelines

Call well in advance to make an appointment to visit with college representatives, especially if you want an interview with an admissions officer, faculty member, or the director of financial aid. It may be difficult to meet with some college representatives and admissions officers between August and December, because they tend to visit high schools during the fall. You can visit on a day when most high schools are closed (e.g., a legal holiday). Make an appointment 3 or 4 months in advance. Some things you should do on your second visit include:

- » Plan to spend enough time to experience "a day in the life of a student."
- » Eat in the student dining halls again.
- » Sit in on at least one class.
- » Spend a night in a dorm room.
- » Spend some time in a student activity center.
- » Ask students why they decided to attend that particular school.

» Read bulletin boards and student newspapers.
» Plan to visit faculty members in academic or arts departments that interest you. Speak with athletic coaches and others who can provide information that will help you make your decision.
» Plan to present final credentials such as musical compositions, portfolios, and evidence of recent achievements.
» When in doubt, ask. No question is unimportant in this process. Always get the name of the person you are talking to in case you have questions at a later time.
» If necessary, speak to the director of financial aid. Ask about merit- or talent-based scholarships.
» Recheck questions written prior to the visit; make sure they are all answered.
» Be sure to double-check the college's policy on the use of test scores such as AP exams and SAT Subject Tests. Some colleges specify the subject tests they require for admission or placement; others allow applicants to choose which tests to take.

The campus visit will:
» provide firsthand information on colleges and what is expected of students;
» allow you to absorb something of the academic, social, and cultural atmosphere of the college;
» provide information about where college students eat, sleep, study, attend classes, and relax;
» permit you to talk with college students and observe their lifestyles;
» provide firsthand information about the community in which a college is located; and
» give you an opportunity to size up the college in light of your personal goals.

The fact is, no matter how great a school looks on paper, it may not be right for you. If the field that interests you is a field in which "connections" are crucial, or if you need to meet and work with people in your field before you graduate, a scholarship from a school that can't provide those opportunities doesn't mean much.

Questions to Ask During a Campus Visit

The following list of suggested questions includes criteria you will find in any good college planning book. It also includes the general and specific questions gifted students should ask when investigating and analyzing colleges. Gifted students who are planning campus visits may wish to use the list to check off categories of personal importance. For example, a student who is primarily interested in the quality of the faculty at the colleges he or she applies to may use the list of questions in that category. Some students may find the list useful when they attempt to dispel myths that accompany college planning decisions: Questions about terms such as *intimate school size, rural pristine setting,* or *selective* may have some surprise answers.

It is important to understand that there are no right or wrong answers. It is your responsibility to learn everything you can about a school you may attend for 4 or more years. No one would expect you to ask every one of the questions that follow, or to use their exact words. The questions are merely meant to guide your thinking as you read the college guides or use college selection software programs, visit campuses, and talk to college students, alumni, faculty, administrators, and others. Select the groups of questions that are important about college to you and your parents and concentrate your questions in those areas.

Questions About the Goals of a College

» What are the implicit and explicit missions and goals of the college or university? Does the school accommodate students who prefer to develop their intellectual abilities and judgment, as well as those who want to train for a specific profession? Does the college provide a climate that encourages students to think clearly and independently, to integrate the disciplines, and to become lifelong learners?

» To what degree does the college or university make students aware that they are connected to a united intellectual and social community? How does the school encourage community service?

» To what degree does the college or university celebrate human diversity and allow for individual differences? What resources exist for gifted students who have disabilities, those from ethnic and multicultural groups, and other historically bypassed groups?

Questions About How a College Does Business

» How does the college or university ease the student's transitions from secondary school, to higher education, to career paths?

» How are students recruited? How does the college expect promotional materials and recruitment strategies to shape student expectations? How do college representatives answer sharply focused questions about admission procedures (e.g., the use of standardized test scores and other student information)?

» How does the college or university show commitment to its enrolled students? Are students involved in governing the school? What resources does the school provide for academic advising, personal counseling, and career counseling?

Questions About a College's Image or Reputation

» If the college or university is prestigious, how is prestige maintained and why do *you* want to attend? Is the college best known for academics? Specific academic areas? Athletics? Does the school have a reputation for producing scholars and statesmen?

» If the school is a relatively small school known for its personal attention to students, is it financially sound? Do alumni provide strong financial support for academic programs? Does the size of the student body indicate stability?

» Is the curriculum stable, or has it varied widely from year to year?

Questions About Demographics and Campus Geography
Location

» Is the school setting urban, rural, or suburban? Urban environments usually provide museums, terrific restaurants, and nightlife. When a town exists primarily because a college or university is there, you might have fewer choices when it comes to concerts and other cultural events.

» What are the specific advantages and disadvantages of each setting?

» What methods of transportation exist if you want to go home on weekends or during brief school breaks? If you want to visit friends at another college? How often might you want to go home?

» What community resources exist near the school? Are there any museums nearby? Any specialty libraries?

» What is the *psychological* distance from home? If you attend a school where getting to transportation (train, plane) takes several hours, the psychological distance might be greater than the actual distance.

» How long will it take for a package to reach you?

» If you have been a part of the same group for a long time, do you need to go to school relatively far from home in order to try new activities and ideas?

Size

» How large are classes in each academic area? How does class size affect the quality and quantity of student participation? For example, are large lectures accompanied by discussion sections, study groups, or some other means of reducing class size so that students can discuss class topics? If the school is relatively small, are prerequisite courses offered every semester?

» How is the campus designed? Is it compact? Spread out? Where are the dormitories in relation to classrooms? How long does it take to get to and from the library? Dining halls? Gymnasium? If the area gets a lot of snow, the daily hike to class or labs might take more time.

» What is the ratio of males to females?

» What is the percentage of culturally diverse students? What ethnic groups are represented?

» What is the percentage of undergraduates?

» What percentage of undergraduates commute?

» Does the school offer student seminars or other ways for students to work and learn together? Do faculty members lead the seminars?

» To what degree does campus size affect the facilities provided for student use? If a school boasts of superior technology and research facilities, who has access to them? Graduate students? Upperclassmen? Everyone who has ability, skill, and interest?

Costs

» What is the real meaning of *private*? *State-supported*? *Heavily endowed*?

» How are fees constructed? What are the added costs: student activity fees, lifestyle expenses, and books? Some textbooks cost more than $100, and the cost increases each year. Does the school bookstore sell used books?

» Are loans, scholarships, student aid, and work-study programs available? To whom? What are the requirements and limitations?

» Does the school provide work choices, or do the students have to find the jobs? Are there businesses outside the

123

school (e.g., stores, restaurants) that offer part-time jobs to students?

Questions About Academic Life
Selectivity

» What is the college's rate of return for its freshman class? One of the best ways to measure a school's quality and the satisfaction of its students is to look at the percentage of students who return after the first year and the percentage of entering students who remain there until graduation. If you have selected a college major, look at the department's graduation rate. Typically, large state schools with an open-door admissions policy lose more students after their first year than smaller schools or those that are highly selective. This will impact class size and the use of facilities.

» How are student admissions folders read and evaluated? What relative weight is assigned to objective and subjective information? To numerical factors, such as GPA, class rank, and standardized tests? To subjective information, such as interviews, essays, presentation of special talents, and extracurricular activities?

» Are there quotas for in-state and out-of-state students? For specific geographic areas? For religious, economic, or ethnic groups? For students whose families are legacies and financial contributors?

» How are AP, ACT, and SAT Subject Test scores used? For credit? For exemption? For placement?

Course Offerings

» What major fields of study are offered?
» How is each academic department ranked?
» What are the number and variety of distribution requirements (required courses)?
» What is the relative level of difficulty in specific academic departments?

» How and when do students select an academic major?

» How are students advised within each academic major?

» Can students select an academic major and retain flexibility to pursue career goals, as well as explore other areas of knowledge?

» How difficult is it to change majors?

» To what degree does each academic department prepare students for economic, social, and technological change?

» What are the maximum and minimum number of courses students may take each semester? How long is a semester?

» Does the school provide opportunities for students to enroll in courses offered by other colleges and universities? Is the school part of a consortium?

» Does the school offer a foreign study program? What are its requirements and/or limitations?

» Are undergraduate students encouraged to do independent research and self-directed study under the guidance of faculty mentors?

» Are students required to complete a thesis or senior seminar prior to graduation? If so, does the school state the purpose of the thesis or seminar?

» Does the school provide opportunities for students to apply what they learn either in or out of the classroom?

» Are students required to bring personal computers? Do students have to bring their own software? Who can use the school's computers? Graduate students? Underclassmen? Any student with ability, skill, and interest? Is the number of terminals sufficient to accommodate students during peak periods?

» Where are the computer terminals located in relation to other campus facilities? What time does the computer lab open and close?

» What percentage of its funds does the school allocate to its library collection? To the library building?

» Is there a sufficient number of copies of required readings and library seats during peak periods?
» Is sufficient laboratory space available to accommodate the students enrolled in laboratory courses?

Academic Atmosphere

» What is the level of competition at the school? Laid back? Cutthroat? What do enrolled students say about competition in classes? If the curriculum is highly rigorous, are you well prepared?
» Does the school have an honors system or code of conduct? If so, how do students feel about it? Are standards enforced consistently?
» How does the school encourage creativity?

Faculty

» Who teaches undergraduates? Professors? Graduate assistants? Who teaches freshmen?
» What does the school expect of its faculty? How does the school encourage and reward faculty?
» What is the primary emphasis of the school? Scholarship? Research? Publications? How is good teaching encouraged? By student evaluations? Peer evaluations?
» How does the school encourage professional growth?
» What do students and faculty members say about the promotion and tenure system?
» What percentage of the faculty are part-time or adjunct instructors who do not have offices on campus?
» When are most faculty members available for student conferences and discussions? Only during office hours? At home? By telephone? Are teachers visible in dining halls and student centers?
» What is the relationship between faculty and students? Are most faculty members available outside of class? Do they respond to inquiries with patience? If not, is there a problem with faculty members and relationships?

>> What opportunities exist for contact with faculty in your desired academic department?

Grading Policies

>> What grading system does the school use? A–F only? Pass/fail? Can the students go ungraded? Are there written evaluations?

Time Structure

>> Does the school operate on the semester system? Quarter system? Trimester system?

>> Does the school offer a minisemester, such as an intense 1-month term in January or May that students can use to improve their grades or enrich their education?

>> How many classroom hours are required each semester to graduate in 4 years?

Questions About Student Life

Orientation Procedures

>> How does the school acquaint freshmen with campus life, rules, and resources?

>> Does the school hold a freshman convocation or have any procedure for celebrating the entrance of each new class?

>> How do freshmen register for classes? Do they meet with an adviser prior to registration?

>> How much assistance can they reasonably expect during the first year? If a student experiences severe academic difficulty, will an adviser call to offer assistance?

Social Structure and Campus Life

>> What extracurricular activities, academic competitions, athletics, and special interest groups are available?

>> Does the community welcome students?

>> Is there an ethnic or religious group in which to take part?

>> How do fraternities and sororities influence campus life?

» Is housing guaranteed?

» To what degree does the school encourage students to share their talents with others? Are faculty and students encouraged to volunteer for community service projects both within and outside of the school?

» To what degree do students participate in campus matters, particularly academic affairs?

» Does the school provide a climate in which all individuals are encouraged to work toward shared objectives?

» How does the school convey the prevailing rules system to students? Are the rules rigid? Loose?

» To what degree does the college tolerate or encourage student activism? Who controls the student newspaper?

» What is the policy on alcohol and substance use and abuse, and what happens to students who break the rules? What about sororities and fraternities?

» What living arrangements does the college offer? Are coed and single-sex dormitories available to all? What is the policy regarding privacy versus open visitation?

» What percentage of the students commute, and where do they live? If the majority of students commute, this will impact campus life. In addition, commuting students may be older than typical college students.

» To what degree does the economic status of the student body influence campus life and/or activities? Are students asked to pay for every event?

» Is the school homogeneous or heterogeneous? If you attend a homogeneous school, you can expect that students will be similar to one another in some important ways. For example, everyone may dress alike because a particular style is popular. If you attend a heterogeneous school, you can expect everyone will do "their own thing." An example of a heterogeneous school is a very large state university. An example of a homogeneous school is a small liberal arts college. Do all students feel comfortable, regardless of lifestyle preference?

» How is the food on campus? Does the food taste good? Is the food good for you? Is there a variety of student dining halls?

» To what degree does the school encourage nonacademic campuswide activities that promote a sense of community?

» What organizations, clubs, and honor societies are available? For socializing? For career planning? For religious practice? Do faculty members attend these organizations on a regular basis?

» Does the school offer planned events on most weekends? If so, what kind of events? Would you attend?

» What provisions exist for student entertainment? On the campus? Off the campus? Is the school a party school? How do the students spend their leisure time?

Campus Security

» Are personal belongings safe if left unattended in dormitory rooms and classrooms?

» What provisions are made to ensure student safety, especially when there is a threat on campus and students should stay inside?

» Is it safe and acceptable to walk from the library to the dormitory alone? If not, what provisions are offered to protect personal safety?

Health

» What provisions does the school offer to assist students with physical and mental health?

» How is the student health center staffed? With nurses only? Are physicians on duty at all times?

» How far is the nearest well-equipped hospital?

» Does the student health center provide a comprehensive health education program and preventive medical advice? Does it provide help with stress? Assistance with personal health questions? Is personal counseling available? If so, what services are provided and what are the qualifications of the staff?

Study Skills
» What facilities are available to students who want to improve their study skills?
» Does the school offer instruction in different study skills in each academic area?

Career Guidance
» How does the school help students choose a career? Get a job? Select a graduate or professional school?
» What are the school's most recent experiences in placing alumni in graduate schools, professional schools, or jobs?
» Are internships and cooperative programs available in specific curricular areas?

Questions for Gifted Students With Disabilities
» How does the school encourage special groups of students to enroll?
» What specific provisions exist for meeting the special academic, physical, and social needs of these students?
» What is the school's retention rate for students with disabilities?

STUDENT ATHLETES: CHOOSING AND VISITING PROSPECTIVE COLLEGES

Student athletes, or at least those who wish to play varsity sports at the collegiate level, have additional considerations when choosing a college. Although a college may recruit you, instead of you seeking out the college, you still need to ensure that you make the right fit for you academically, emotionally, and socially. You should make sure that you follow the same principles set forth for other students in this book, asking relevant questions, visiting colleges, experiencing all you can on campus, and taking time to make a good, sound decision. There are, however, some very specific things college-bound student athletes must do in the college planning process.

When you first begin to wonder if you might be eligible for collegiate-level sports, visit the National Collegiate Athletic Association's (NCAA) website (http://www.ncaa.org). The NCAA governs all varsity-level intercollegiate sports at more than 1,200 colleges nationwide, and its website provides student athletes with plenty of good information about the rules and procedures behind the athlete recruiting process. It's also a good idea to download a copy of the organization's free *Guide for the College-Bound Student-Athlete* (NCAA, 2013–2014) from its website.

If you wish to participate in varsity sports during your first year of college, you *must* first register with the NCAA Initial-Eligibility Clearinghouse, an organization that will determine your eligibility for participation in NCAA sports. This organization looks at each student's high school academic records, ACT or SAT scores, and whether the student qualifies as an amateur athlete. To participate in college-level sports, students must be determined to be an amateur by the NCAA Clearinghouse; in other words, the organization will review your records for issues such as a contract with a professional sports team, receiving a salary for participating in athletics, preferential treatment based on your athletics reputation, and benefits from prospective professional sports agents (NCAA, 2013–2014).

Students who are determined to be eligible for varsity sports by the Clearinghouse can then move on to the next steps: visiting and/or being recruited by college sports programs. It's important for student-athletes to review the recruiting regulations for college sports as laid out in the *Guide for the College-Bound Student-Athlete* (NCAA, 2013–2014). A number of rules and regulations apply to this process, and it's important to make sure you follow each one carefully. Many schools encourage students to send videotapes of their high school playing time to the prospective sport's recruiting office. Coaches and assistants review these tapes often, and, although a coach will not make a decision to recruit you based solely on your taped performance, the videotape may alert him or her to your abilities, making you a potential recruit he or she had not seen or considered beforehand.

Often, college coaches pay close attention to various high schools' performance each season. Coaches know the area they recruit from well, visiting schools in their region often, reading newspapers and Internet recounts of the local sports, and reviewing tapes of student-athletes who play in their regions. It's likely that if you are a standout athlete at a top-performing school, coaches from several universities are already aware of your abilities. However, no matter your performance record, reputation, or abilities, the recruiting process remains the same; NCAA rules do not allow for any special or preferential treatment for college athletes at any time. The recruiting process includes several important events, including the initial contact, the evaluation period, and the official visit.

Contact is a term used by NCAA to describe any time when a coach has any face-to-face contact with you or your parents off of the college's campus. During the *contact period*, a college coach may have in-person contact with you and/or your parents on or off of the college's campus; this means the coach may watch you play or visit you at your high school, he or she may write or telephone you, and you and your parents may visit a college campus during this time. The *evaluation* takes place when a college evaluates your athletic and academic ability, either by visiting your high school or watching you practice or compete. However, during the *evaluation period*, the coach may watch you play, but he or she cannot have any in-person contact with you or your parents off of the college campus. Another important part of the recruiting process is the *official visit*, which occurs any time you and your parents visit the college, and the college pays for your expenses, such as transportation and meals (NCAA, 2013–2014).

varsity sports like volleyball and softball are also offered
ports, along with others like rugby, lacrosse, and cycling),
st large universities have very competitive intramural
rograms (where clubs, student-organized teams, and
ompete against one another) for sports like flag football,
ll, three-on-three basketball, slow pitch softball, and soc-
ure and ask about these various athletic opportunities
e on campus during your campus visit.

These are only a few of the specific t⟩ the recruiting process; for more inforr⟩ *Guide for the College-Bound Student-At⟩*

While gathering information abo⟩ colleges, there are certain specific que⟩ coaches to help you make a sound d⟩ Some questions you should conside⟩ 2013–2014):

> » What position(s) will I play on⟩
> » What expectations do you⟩ conditioning?
> » How would you best describe t⟩
> » How many credit hours sho⟩ season?
> » Are there restrictions in scl⟩ practice?
> » What is a typical day like for a ⟩
> » Must student athletes live on c⟩
> » What kind of athletic scholars⟩ do they cover? What do they n⟩
> » Under what circumstances w⟩ reduced or canceled?
> » What scholarship money is ava⟩ is over to help me complete my⟩ athletes are only eligible for 4 ye⟩ such as many engineering prog⟩ years to complete. If you are thi⟩ might take you longer than 4 ye⟩ good question to ask.)

Again, if you're considering playing s⟩ **134** thing to do is to check out the NCAA's w⟩ mation, rules, and regulations. If you ar⟩ sity team, but don't want to give up sport⟩ Many schools operate university-gover⟩ that compete against other nearby schoo⟩

ditiona⟩ as club⟩ and m⟩ sports⟩ dorms⟩ volleyb⟩ cer. Be⟩ availab⟩

5 THE APPLICATION PROCESS
What Do I Have That They Want?

At this point you know a lot about colleges and have thought about where you might like to spend the next 4 years. You have an idea about your traits and characteristics, and what that means in respect to "the list" you have selected. It doesn't matter whether the list is 10 colleges or 20. Congratulations, you have a start.

Chapter 5 completes the college matching process by answering the questions "What do I have that they want?" and "How can I show them my 'best' self in the application process?" In addition, this chapter covers the final steps of the college planning process: the application, including the presentation of credentials (grades, GPA, standardized test scores, including AP tests from 11th grade if available, class rank if available, and special awards). If you have been involved in an IB program and you are academically successful, explain. Don't assume that everyone is familiar with IB courses like "Theory of Knowledge." Eventually you will want to concentrate on presenting activities and awards to make you "come alive" on paper. The rest of the process—interviewing and writing an essay—will come later, as will applying for financial aid and making acceptance decisions. Academic performance is the most important. If an admissions counselor believes that you will not succeed academically, your application will get no further.

The application process is discussed from two points of view: that of the multipotential gifted student, who may be able to make rational choices, but whose options are infinite; and that of the admissions officer, who may have to select the freshman class from a wide range of highly qualified applicants. Keep in mind the following:

» If a student decides to attend college early, parents should assess the student's ability to live away from the family, establish social relationships in college, and set long-term goals. The pros and cons of attending an online university should be weighed, along with other possibilities such as early entrance programs.

» There is no such thing as *the perfect school*, and the way the student addresses the application process may be a critical factor determining acceptance or rejection.

» Admission officers are human, with a job to do. They have to "sell the college" to students who might be a good match for school offerings, and then attract the students who will be a good match for the school. That differs from year to year and school to school.

» Colleges are usually looking for a well-rounded, diverse student body. What does that mean? Students frequently join every activity available in an effort to appear well rounded, but colleges would rather see fewer activities and concentrated commitment to one or two. When the college decides on the incoming freshman class, there will be students with a variety of skills. There will be musicians; sports enthusiasts; academic super achievers; students from rural areas, the city, and suburbs; and students from many income levels, countries, and cultures—in other words, a well-rounded, diverse student body.

» The admit-deny decision is *not* an evaluation of a person's worth as a student and as a person.

COLLEGE ADMISSION PREP CAMPS AND INDEPENDENT COLLEGE PLANNING CONSULTANTS

Travel to Tufts University or UCLA during the summer and you will see a college admission prep camp in action. College admission has become so competitive that some parents and students are no longer willing to approach it without professional help. Talking to an admissions counselor, reading college publications, or practicing the SAT or ACT at home is not enough to reduce the angst for some families, especially those with students applying to highly selective colleges.

Students need more refined tools if they are to apply to a highly selective school. An increasingly popular solution is college admission prep camps (Hansen, n.d.). They are run by private companies and college counseling organizations and are scattered throughout the nation. Students can enroll in a prep camp and get individual instruction on their college essay, take an SAT or ACT prep course, receive one-on-one college counseling, and get help with study skills and time management. However, this approach does not come cheap. The college admission prep camps run by Education Unlimited at eight campuses throughout the nation cost more than $4,000 for 11 days. Room and board at a residential camp? That's more than $6,000. Education Unlimited is adding online courses in topics such as taking the SAT. Most of the private companies host small groups of students who spend 12 hours a day, every day, taking classes or receiving individual help on college planning. Most students have no idea how to approach the admissions process, and with an average student-counselor ratio of 500 to 1 in public schools, they are unlikely to get what they need from overworked guidance counselors. When exploring these camps, make sure you are getting the return you are looking for.

Another approach to the college planning process is engaging the services of a private counselor to provide one-on-one counseling. *Independent counselors* and *educational consultants* are two different terms used to describe a counselor/adviser outside of the school setting who assists students and parents with the college admission process for a fee. Usually, they prefer to begin a program no later than a student's sophomore year, and work with the student until his or her applications have been sent, although most people begin later. You should always ask for qualifications, including personal references. And you should interview more than one consultant, because you are looking for a knowledgeable person who will "click" with your son or daughter.

Independent counselors spend time visiting colleges and universities and frequently have relationships with admissions staff members. Experienced counselors often know how to help students market their strengths and "come alive" on paper. Also, they are usually on mailing lists and have access to information others don't have. For example, one U.S. college takes great pride in its bagpipe band. One year, most of the band members graduated, and the university sent out a notice that they would award a full tuition, room, and board scholarship to students who were qualified academically and had some expertise playing a bagpipe. Such unusual, but rewarding, information given to private consultants and college counselors can pay off, and may make it well worth the cost of hiring outside advisers.

Before you invest in a private counselor or camp, you may want to become familiar with the process, as well as local resources. Only then can you decide whether your teen needs outside help.

A LOOK AT THE APPLICATION

We begin with a look at the application and the process by which candidates are evaluated. Two kinds of information are required on the typical college application form: objective and subjective. Objective information includes biographical data, information on academic performance, standardized test scores such as SATs or ACTs, AP or IB classes or exam grades, and additional numerical information. Subjective information includes the presentation of extracurricular activities, recommendations, the essay and/or personal statement, and a personal interview. Depth and scope of extracurricular activity are preferred to a "laundry list" of activities. Colleges are particularly interested in a student's initiative, leadership ability, indication of community service, and commitment.

When the academic credentials of two applicants are roughly equal, subjective information and the student's method of presentation become deciding factors. (Sometimes a student's geographic location, the school his or her parents attended, or particular talents can tip the balance.)

At this point, it's a good idea to begin organizing your application materials. Getting organized before you begin the procedure of applying to schools can ease some of the stress and tension you may feel later on. Knowing you have everything in order and under control can be very helpful when multiple application deadlines spring up at once. The application organizer in Figure 9 can help. You can make your own spreadsheet using Microsoft Excel or any spreadsheet program.

You will also want to create a folder for use in the application process, containing the following items:

> » recommendations from adult leaders of special programs in which you participated during ninth, 10th, and 11th grades;
> » transcripts and course descriptions from out-of-school courses;
> » your application organizer, placed in a spot where it's easy to access (such as stapled to the front inside cover) and where you can see how you are progressing; and
> » a calendar of deadlines for *everything*, which should be stapled to the cover.

139

School Name:			
College Applications	**Date**	**Date**	**Date**
Application deadline			
Essay completed			
Application form completed			
Application mailed			
Notification date			
Financial Aid Applications			
Financial aid application deadline			
FAFSA mailed			
Completed PROFILE registration process			
PROFILE form mailed			
College's financial aid application mailed			
Recommendation Letters			
1. Gave recommendation form to: _____			
Writer mailed form or returned it to me			
Sent thank-you note			
2. Gave recommendation form to: _____			
Writer mailed form or returned it to me			
Sent thank-you note			
3. Gave recommendation form to: _____			
Writer mailed form or returned it to me			
Sent thank-you note			
High School Transcripts			
Gave transcript to counselor			

Figure 9. Application organizer.

School Name:			
High School Transcripts	**Date**	**Date**	**Date**
Form mailed			
Gave midyear school report form to counselor			
Form mailed			
Test Scores			
Requested that score reports be sent to colleges			
		Score	
SAT			
SAT Subject Tests			
ACT			
AP exams			
IB			
Other			
Other			
Other			

Figure 9. Continued.

Colleges look favorably upon transcripts showing increasing academic rigor during 4 years of high school. A quirk in the transcript (e.g., an atypical course or low grade in a challenging academic course) should be accompanied by an explanation, particularly if the event occurs during 11th or 12th grade. This is tricky, because if your explanation doesn't sound credible, you don't want to call attention to it. An example of a situation requiring explanation is a period of illness during which a student falls far behind in his or her work and receives a poor or failing grade. Explanations are also useful if a student experiences family problems, overcomes difficulties, or maintains grades in spite of difficulties. You should address these situations in an essay or personal statement. If your transcript looks like a roller coaster or if you have a low grade in an academically challenging course, you need to explain. See the example below.

> Jorge missed more than half of the first semester of 12th grade because of illness. His teachers cooperated with him and he was able to keep up with the work, except for that in calculus. The calculus teacher was unwilling to prepare work to send home. When he returned to school, he received F's in calculus, but decided to stay in the class despite the unlikely possibility of raising his grade. His reason, he explained to his family, was that he was eventually going to need calculus, and he could learn more in that class than he could learn in a study hall, which was his only other choice. When he applied to colleges, he chose colleges that provided an opportunity to make a personal statement and he explained his situation. He was offered admission to four selective schools. The schools that rejected his application were those that conducted their initial screening by computer. His calculus grade knocked him out of competition for those schools, one of which was his "safety school."

The parts of the application should fit together to provide a common theme. Recommendations should support and be consistent with both the academic record and what the student says about him- or herself. Again, any quirk should be explained. For example, high SAT/ACT scores combined with a relatively low GPA or a high GPA and low SAT/ACT scores provide an inconsistent picture of an applicant. They may suggest a problem (e.g., high ability but low motivation) to an admissions officer and need to be addressed in the application package or interview.

Documentation of activities may be critical to the admissions process. To document activities, students may, for example, enter a contest, submit work for publication, keep a scientific journal, or keep a notebook of artistic works. Active participation in a highly competitive individual or team sport should always be documented. But know when to play it safe. When considering the use of gimmicks or attention-grabbers, be careful to distinguish between those that cause you to stick out and those that help you to stand out.

Entering national competitions and contests is one way to help you stand out, while documenting your interests. The Johns Hopkins University Center for Talented Youth website provides a list of competitions that is kept up to date.

The following examples illustrate ways of documenting interests and proficiency.

Julie was a capable, academically successful student who aspired to attend a highly competitive college. At an early age, she became interested in race walking. She spent her leisure time perfecting this skill, but it never occurred to her to document her interest. Her counselor discovered Julie's interest and suggested that she enter a race walking competition. Much to Julie's surprise, she placed 25th in a regional competition. The contest added another dimension to her leisure interest and gave her an edge in the college application process. The competition showed commitment.

Jon was a mathematically gifted student, but his grades were average because he spent most of his time creating and constructing puzzles of every variety imaginable. Jon explained his interest in a personal statement attached to his application and submitted a puzzle with the application. His puzzle consisted of some wood strips and a question. He asked whether anyone could construct a kinetic geometric model showing the "interpenetration and duality of the cube and the octahedron." He did not include the solution. The admissions officer contacted Jon to ask him how to solve the puzzle.

The Common Application

Counselors and parents may find that gifted students suddenly decide to apply to a particular college and have not sent for the application. In such a case, the Common Application or the lesser known Universal College Application may meet the needs of the student. The Universal College Application (https://www.universalcollegeapp.com/) includes a list of schools that participate. The theory behind it is the same—one application going to several schools. Some schools accept both generic applications, but most don't. You have to choose. Some schools require students to use one of the two and do not provide an application.

The Common Application is a standardized application that is accepted by approximately 500, mostly private, selective colleges and universities for admission to their undergraduate programs. Students complete one Common Application form, photocopy it, and send the form to any of the participating colleges. The procedure simplifies the college application process and eliminates duplication of effort. To further simplify the process, you can use the Common Application website (https://www.commonapp.org) to complete your forms and submit them electronically or in hard copy. Or, download PDF forms to complete onscreen or manually, then print and mail the hard copy to the school to which you're applying. Be sure to use the latest version. For the 2013–2014 application cycle, the Common Application unveiled a major technological overhaul as well as some significant changes to its content. One of the biggest changes is the essay prompts, which may vary somewhat from year to year. The paper application may be retired in 2014. You will save time by using the Common Application, but it may not always be the best choice. A student's individuality will come through most clearly when he or she chooses the avenues of communication with care. So, before you use the Universal College Application or the Common Application, compare it with each school's application form.

Electronic Applications

The college planning process has been thoroughly infused with technology. Schools distribute most of their information via website, including college costs, the college profile (e.g., SAT/

ACT scores of current students), the course catalog, and detailed admission information. Schools receive more than half their applications electronically. There are usually two ways to do this: (1) download and print the application, complete it by hand, and mail it by postal service; or (2) complete the application online and submit it electronically through the college's website. When you choose to submit electronically, print your completed application so that your counselor or parents can proofread it. If your high school is sending your information, check with counselors a month ahead of the deadline. Counselors may be responsible for hundreds of students, and you don't want to be the one who "falls through the cracks." Many large state schools have their own applications online for students to complete and send. They may provide a form to input a transcript. Pay close attention to this step because your application is incomplete without your transcript.

Keep a paper copy of everything you send so that if something happens to your electronic application, you will have a backup that you can mail before the deadline. Then, follow up with a phone call or e-mail to make sure your application arrived and is intact. Using an electronic application process is great for some people, but you have to be careful to send the application well ahead of the deadline. Although technology has come a long way, there are no guarantees. One year, a university's server crashed as a result of the onslaught of applications sent electronically just minutes before the deadline. On another occasion, an Internet service provider interpreted acceptance letters from a highly selective school as spam and deleted them. So if you submit your application electronically, be sure to follow up.

HOW CANDIDATES
ARE EVALUATED

The following scene typifies an admissions office at a small highly selective college or larger university. The difference is the number of people needed to read applications.

The admissions counselor is sitting at his desk, which is piled high with application folders. He has read 40 applications today. It is now 10 p.m., and he would like to go home. Instead, he takes the next folder off the pile and reviews it as always, with no knowledge of the student—what the student is like, what the student has accomplished, what the student hopes to achieve, and what the student can contribute to the college. The admissions officer may spend no more than 5 or 10 minutes looking at the application during this first reading. The admissions officer will first look at the name of the student's school district to see whether he is familiar with the quality of the education provided there. He will then look at the student's high school profile to see if the high school has a challenging academic program, and finally will check the student's academic performance—courses taken and grades earned. He follows this pattern because when a college accepts a student, it gambles on the student's chances of succeeding at the school. A student who performs consistently well all through high school is a much lower risk than one whose performance has been erratic. Even though a student's record may identify him or her as gifted (or enrolled in a special program), colleges will evaluate the student's credentials in the same manner as those of all other students.

In some instances, computers perform initial reviews. Applicant data is entered into a computer formula and the computer recommends whether admission should be accepted or denied. The admission committee looks at the application and the computer-generated data before making a final decision.

This process is a distinct disadvantage to a gifted student whose academic numerical credentials—GPA, class rank, or standardized test scores—are not reflective of the student's high ability and potential. It may also be a problem for students who are homeschooled.

What Do Admissions Officers Look for?

Academic Performance

A student's academic performance consists of several factors: grade point average, class rank, and academic rigor. When looking at your grade point average and class rank, a school will ask: How good are the student's grades, and where does the student stand compared to classmates? When checking for academic rigor, an admissions officer will seek evidence of superior ability in the form of honors, an IB Program, or AP courses. Some colleges ignore honors or GT classes because they are of unknown quality. Students should be alert to the difference between state academic requirements for high school graduation and requirements for admission to a selective college. The most selective colleges are interested in evidence of high motivation and achievement—that is, high grades in very demanding courses. Taking AP courses demonstrates that the student is capable of performing at a high level of academic proficiency. AP grades of 3, 4, or 5 *may* be accepted for exemption from a university's required freshman courses and/or for college credit. Students, you should check a college's AP/IB policy. You should not just assume that you will receive transcript credit or place out of freshman-level classes for your test scores. Academic rigor consists of the following elements:

» *Depth* in areas such as foreign languages and mathematics. Studying one language for 6 years is better than studying two languages for 3 years apiece.
» *Quality.* Did the student take four or five major subjects each year (English, mathematics, science, history, language) or a variety of nonacademic or elective courses

(e.g., business law, fashion merchandising, culinary arts, study hall)? Course descriptions should reflect the rigor of each course. If a high school does not include course descriptions and a profile of school credentials with college applications, and course titles do not accurately reflect quality, the student or counselor should attach an explanation to the transcript. School credentials include factors like the number of students who take AP courses or complete an IB program and the number of students who are eligible for free lunch because of their family's low income.

» *Balance.* Did the student take a broad curriculum (mathematics and science, history, and English courses), or concentrate too heavily in one area?

» *Trends.* Are the student's grades gradually improving, or growing weaker each year? Recent performance is the most important indicator of the student's current level of ability and motivation.

One dean of admissions was asked whether he would prefer to see a C in calculus or an A in a less rigorous course. This is one of the most common questions asked at college information sessions. Of course he replied, "An A in calculus." The audience tittered and the real question remains unanswered. One answer might be: If the student takes rigorous courses in other disciplines, a C in calculus is better than a higher grade in a relatively easy mathematics course. Although the dean sidestepped the question, his response indicated that students should take the most rigorous courses offered by their high school. If the student's high school offers AB or BC calculus, then the student should take calculus, unless taking an advanced math course will send his or her GPA plunging downward. So one issue is GPA. A second issue is the quality of the student's other courses. If a student took several AP courses that semester and chose to take a less rigorous math course, earning an A in that course, the choice might ultimately be a good one.

Standardized Test Scores

Standardized test scores supplement high school transcripts and permit an admissions officer to compare all applicants with one standard. These tests share a common characteristic: They are timed and yield a standardized score. At least half of all students take the SAT twice—in the spring of their junior year and in the fall of their senior year. Most students also improve their score the second time around. The College Board may use several versions of the test on a given day, but all versions will be comparable. For the SAT Subject Tests, most students take them toward the end of their junior year or at the beginning of their senior year. In general, you should take tests such as World History, Biology E/M, Chemistry, or Physics as soon as possible after completing the course in the subject. The verbal and mathematics portions are multiple-choice tests. When the PSATs and SATs were revised, more emphasis was placed on critical thinking skills in both the verbal and mathematical sections (College Board, n.d.b). The SAT now includes an essay portion requiring students to take a position on an issue and use reasoning and examples to support their position (College Board, n.d.a). At the same time, the ACT added a writing test that measures writing skills emphasized in high school English classes and in entry-level college composition courses.

Selective schools may emphasize SAT Subject Test scores. Students may take one, two, or three tests each testing session. The only exception is for listening tests—students may take one listening test and two other subject tests. If you are taking a course in which you are doing quite well, consider taking a subject test if one is offered. Do not wait until your senior year to do so; you may forget what you have learned. In addition, you may want to take more than three subject tests, and, if you wait until senior year, this will be impossible. The SAT and SAT Subject Tests must be taken on separate testing dates.

Schools will vary in whether they require subject tests and in how many applicants are required to take. Rather than generate extensive lists of schools and required tests, you should check each college that interests you. In order to be sure you are meeting all requirements, check each individual school's testing requirements and plan ahead. A student who plans to take the SAT and three subject tests could take the SAT in May of his or her junior year, two subject tests in June, the SAT for a second time in October of his or her senior year, and the remaining subject tests in November. That will leave the December test date to repeat any test on which a higher score is desired.

Many websites offer students the opportunity to download, print, and take a free, full-length practice test. Some offer a review and skills report, and explanations to all test answers so students can see how and why they earned a particular score. The test preparation company Kaplan has a teenager-friendly answer to practicing for the SATs—test prep software that runs on handheld computers like the iPod and smartphones.

Some colleges prefer to see scores from the ACT. Like the SAT, the ACT assesses high school students' general educational development and their ability to complete college-level work. Unlike the SAT, the ACT includes multiple-choice tests that cover four skill areas: English, mathematics, reading, and science (ACT, n.d.a). The added 30-minute writing test is optional and measures skill in planning and writing a short essay. Each section of the test is scored from 1 to 36; then, those four section scores are averaged for a composite score. The maximum composite score a student can achieve on the ACT is 36, a score earned by approximately one percent of the 1.2 million test takers. Students who take the optional writing test receive all of the same scores that students who do not take the writing test receive. In addition, students who take the writing test receive a scaled score, ranging from 1–36, that reflects their performance on the writing test and the English Test combined, and constructive feedback on their writing in the form of reader comments (ACT, n.d.b).

Colleges vary in their use of standardized test scores. Some schools, believing that SAT and ACT scores predict college grades, use scores as one criterion for admission decisions. Other schools place primary emphasis on high school academic achievement and AP/IB scores and then look at subjective information such as the student essay. Students should ask college representatives how the various scores and tests are used in their college's admissions process.

Extracurricular Activities

Seth was interested in engineering. He knew that the field was changing, so during 10th grade he researched different types of engineering. He was fascinated with forensic engineering professionals who evaluate crime scene evidence to narrow the search for a criminal. He knew he wanted to be of service to humanity and thought about the possibility of becoming a pharmaceutical engineer, one who perhaps discovers a vaccine for a disease. He also liked designing things and was interested in robotics and aerodynamics. During 11th grade, he volunteered in a laboratory where vaccines were developed, realizing in the process that he felt good about himself and the problems that the scientists let him work on. Seth worked in the laboratory for the next 2 years. He applied to highly selective colleges and was accepted by most. He had good grades in rigorous science and math courses, but that wasn't all. The admissions officers saw that Seth had a track record in his chosen field and he had conducted some independent research, qualities that gave him an edge in a highly competitive admissions process.

Imagine the following scene: After the application deadline, an admissions committee reviews all applications by looking at each one for about 10 minutes. They know that they can accept about one student in six, so the first thing they do is divide the applications into three stacks. Some applications are immediately placed in a rejection pile because the students' academic credentials do not indicate future success at the school in question. But then, faced with a pile of acceptable applicants, the admissions officer picks a folder and says, "What makes you so special? Why should I accept you?" He is going to try to determine how the applicant spends his or her time outside the classroom and what these activities say about the applicant.

Most selective colleges ask students to list, describe, and sometimes comment on the significance of their extracurricular activities. They are interested in depth of commitment, personal initiative, originality, leadership ability, and evidence of a social conscience. If the student has had problems, they want to see resilience, the ability to work through problems and overcome them. An applicant does not need an exhaustive list to have an impact. In fact, membership in several student organizations is less impressive than a major contribution to one organization or activity. This means that you do not have to hold an office in every club or be captain of every team. Admissions officers want to gauge the quality of a student's performance in an activity. They want to see whether or not you can pursue an activity and acquire expertise in it. They also look for leadership and evidence that you have shared your talents and expertise with others. Extracurricular activities demonstrate skills and abilities that cannot be seen on a student's transcript. This information rounds out an application.

Some students pursue solitary interests; they might be computer hackers, basement scientists, or midnight poets. Your particular interest will be easier to discuss if it is documented in some way. You can avoid a last-minute flurry of activity by keeping a journal or blog of your progress, keeping a notebook of your poems, entering contests, or finding some method to convey to colleges that your interest in an activity did not begin and end when you realized you needed to include activities on your application. Well-rounded activities indicate a student's interest in a variety of endeavors, but intense concentration in one or two areas, if properly documented, is more likely to be impressive, especially if the activity is related to a student's career goals.

For example, when asked on the college application to "describe the importance of a sport or sports to you and discuss what you feel you've gained from participation in sports," a student admitted to a highly selective college replied, in part, with the following statement:

> It was very important for me to get involved in sports when I started high school. I was short for my age and somewhat shy. To be part of a team and to get to know and trust your teammates at a time when you need all the friends you can get was invaluable. As a freshman, making the freshman basketball team really helped me fit in and feel comfortable in high school. I discovered you don't have to be the team superstar to make being there worthwhile. At 14, I was only 5' 2" and saw very little court time, but it was probably more rewarding for me to be there than my taller teammates and to have accomplished my preseason goal of making the team. I was certainly the shortest one trying out for the team that year, and I was very nervous, yet I never gave up and I never stopped hustling. Making the team that year gave me the confidence to do other things that made me nervous.

The rest of the student's statement briefly described the frustrations, trials, and tribulations encountered through 4 years of high school athletics and clearly indicated what he learned from his years of participation in different sports. Additional personal statements in his application indicated that the student was a successful problem solver. He was also academically successful.

Technology has introduced a new dimension to documenting extracurricular activities. Applicants can produce multimedia DVDs illustrating their skills and abilities. However, media presentation of skills is effective only if it demonstrates an aspect of the student's ability that cannot be demonstrated in any other way and relates to the student's ability to perform in college. Using multimedia does not necessarily demonstrate the capacity to be original and creative; it is a means to an end rather than an end in itself. The following examples illustrate this point.

Josh was an expert windsurfer. The admissions office received a professional-quality DVD showing Josh successfully navigating his way through relatively difficult surf. Although it was interesting, the presentation had little impact on the deliberations of the admissions committee. If, however, Josh added a narrative describing the way windsurfing relates to his interest and abilities in physics, he would have provided necessary meaning to his interest and credentials.

Dora's primary strengths were her sense of humor and artistic ability. She was often bored in class and drew satirical cartoons while teachers lectured. When Dora applied to selective colleges, she capitalized on her abilities by producing an animated cartoon. Her theme, school politics, cast some of her teachers in a rather poor light, but it reflected her ability to use technology effectively, as well as her ability to cope with some negative educational experiences through her sense of humor. Counselor recommendations provided consistency by discussing Dora's sense of humor and ability to deal with diverse situations.

Dora was interested in animation and marketing and applied to a college that was known for nurturing students interested in technology and business. Because Dora chose an appropriate college, the admissions officer understood her experiences and her sense of humor as portrayed in the presentation. He predicted that she would blossom in the university's environment. The admissions committee was impressed with Dora's honesty and creativity. The submission, then, made a difference.

Submitting material that provides evidence of talent can be tricky. Admissions officers are flooded with DVDs, portfolios, and home-baked bread. Talent definitely counts, especially in the arts. However, students should ask whether or not the college will accept supplementary material and how they can best present extracurricular activities and special talents. Any method that demonstrates the student's ability to perform in college and adds substance and consistency to the application is desirable.

Students who plan to major in the arts should send performance resumes with their applications. A performance resume is not just a list of places you performed, but rather throughout the resume an arts/drama student needs to show growth in one or two areas.

When the student, guidance counselor, and parents agree to send supporting material, care must be taken in the presentation of that material:

» Send evidence, not testimony.

» Submit the best work in a concise form. Keep it short and to the point.

» Be sure that the supplementary material adds something to the application that cannot be illustrated in any other way, and that it demonstrates, in some way, the student's ability to succeed at the school. This does not mean that a student should submit an application with only a simple description of activities; it simply means that evaluation and informed judgment should guide the presentation of material.

» When in doubt, spell it out. Don't use acronyms or abbreviations. The person reading your application may not understand the terms.

When highly selective colleges decide between two very qualified students who are on par academically, the creative presentation of extracurricular activities, the quality of recommendations, the essay or personal statement, the interview, and other written material can each make a difference.

Community Service

Admissions officers know that an altruistic student, one who has contributed to community life without regard for compensation, is more likely to contribute to campus life, be academically successful, and form a long-term attachment to the college or university. Therefore, volunteer activities should be documented in the application. One example is a talent in a particular sport in which the student participates competitively and coaches young children after school. In such a case, a letter of recommendation from the person who supervised the student's coaching should be in the applicant's folder. Another example might be contributing expertise in developing computer programs; the student may have shared this talent by writing programs that helped a social agency save some money. In this case, a letter of recommendation from the agency director or treasurer should be in the file. A student who volunteers solely to have it included on a resume is wasting an opportunity.

PERSONAL RECOMMENDATIONS

By the time you ask teachers, counselors, and other adults for recommendations, you should have a few recommendations in your file that were written by people who were leaders of summer programs and other activities you attended. Do not include people who didn't get to know you well or who might say something negative.

Effective recommendations answer the question, "What can you tell us about this student that will help us make a decision?" You should ask your counselors and teachers to provide evidence that distinguishes you from other equally qualified candidates and creates a complete and credible picture of you in the mind of an admissions officer. Ask for recommendations from teachers and others who know you well and are likely to take the time to write thoughtful comments. Ask for a recommendation from a teacher in the field in which you may wish to major, preferably a teacher who is genuinely interested in your future. Be sure to ask for recommendations well in advance (several weeks) of the deadline. Provide stamped envelopes that are preaddressed to the colleges, and be sure to thank the teacher. Inform him or her of the colleges' decisions.

In some cases, a recommendation can be used to explain quirks in the student's transcript. The following example illustrates this point.

> Lisa was identified as gifted in elementary school. When she entered ninth grade, she was assigned to rigorous courses and earned A's and B's. Her sophomore year yielded the same results. When Lisa reached 11th grade, teacher expectations changed. As a result, Lisa's midsemester grades in two academic courses were a C and a D. Lisa talked with her parents and decided to confront the problem with private tutoring and extra study. She also dropped out of some of her extracurricular activities. By the end of 11th grade, she earned B's in both subjects. When Lisa applied to selective colleges, her counselor wrote a recommendation that explained how Lisa overcame her problem. A teacher recommendation presented a picture of a highly gifted student who, when confronted with a problem, faced the situation realistically, set goals, and accomplished her mission.

Counselor Recommendations

Counselors who are responsible for more than 500 students would like to know each student well, but that's just not possible. If your guidance counselor does not know you well, make an appointment to discuss your college plans and goals. The following questions are just suggestions as to what information students can give their guidance counselor to use when writing a recommendation. This information may be helpful to your teachers as well.

Counselor recommendations are most effective when they are specific and say what the student does that reflects his or her intellectual ability and growth: depth and breadth of extracurricular involvement; personal characteristics such as initiative, creativity, and leadership capacity; and generosity of spirit. Students, provide your counselors with answers to the following questions and ideas to help them write a recommendation letter for you.

Intellectual and Academic Development

1. To what extent have you taken advantage of academic choices available to you?
2. What course was the most difficult for you, and why? Why did you take that course?
3. How many nonrequired books do you read in a typical month? Year?
    *   What type of nonrequired reading do you enjoy, and why?
    *   Who is your favorite literary character, and why?

4. What else can you think of that has influenced your thinking?
    *   a particular movie?
    *   a cultural event?
    *   an academic competition?
    *   a particular teacher?
    *   a particular mentor?
    *   travel?
    *   a summer experience?

5. Have you taken any academic courses that may not be listed on your transcript? When and where?
6. Are you involved in any artistic or creative activity or intellectual pursuit that is not reflected in your folder, and do you have samples of your work? For example, are you
    *   a basement scientist?
    *   a computer hacker?
    *   a midnight poet?
    *   a composer of music or song lyrics?
    *   a puzzle creator?
    *   a photographer?

Extracurricular Activities

1. List the extracurricular activities you have been involved in. Describe the length of time, depth, and breadth of your involvement. Can you rank your activities according to importance?
2. Have you received any prizes or honors?
3. What positions of leadership have you held?
4. Can you explain your methods of leadership?
5. How did you get results? Did you command? Cajole? Ask?
6. What have you gained from your extracurricular activity? How has it influenced your life?
7. Have you participated in any volunteer activity where you shared your talents? When and where did you volunteer? What did you do to share your talents?

Personal Information

1. Have you had to overcome any problems, difficulties, or disabilities? If so, how did you overcome the problem and what motivated you?
2. How much free time do you have each day and week, and how do you use your free time?
3. How hard have you had to work to achieve your accomplishments?
4. How academically prepared are you for college? How emotionally prepared? Do you feel prepared for the independence available on most college campuses?
5. What makes you unique, compared to your friends?
6. What do you see as the major problem in the United States today? In your state? In your high school? Can you make suggestions as to how to solve any of these problems?
7. What do you see yourself doing in 20 years? In 10 years? In 5 years? In 6 months?

Teacher Recommendations

Securing strong teacher recommendations is important, especially when the teacher can talk about your growth and development in an academic subject. Colleges prefer recommendations from teachers you had in junior or senior year. If you are a highly talented and skilled student in the arts or in sports and plan to major in the area of your talent or play a sport at the college level, you will probably need a letter of reference from someone outside school who is qualified to judge your level of talent. A letter of reference should be written on the person's own stationery and sent to the colleges. You will not be able to upload it to the Common or Universal Application. Be sure to:

- » Ask teachers and others well in advance, at least 4 to 6 weeks ahead of the deadline. Inform the person of the deadline, especially if you are applying Early Decision or Early Action. (Colleges vary.)
- » Ask teachers and others who know you well. If a person agrees to write a recommendation, make an appointment to explain your college plans; that is, where you are applying and the areas that interest you. Provide this information in writing.
- » Provide teachers and others with stamped, addressed envelopes.
- » Be sure to thank the person and keep him or her informed of the colleges' decisions.

The following guidelines may be helpful to give to your teachers when you ask for recommendations. The guidelines, as well as the sample recommendation that follows (see Figure 10), were contributed by a Virginia AP English teacher.

- » Many colleges provide standard forms for evaluations. If you decide not to use a form, make sure that your letter of recommendation contains all the information requested.

» Teacher recommendations are most effective when they say what the student does that reflects his or her intellectual ability and growth, creativity, and generosity of spirit.

» Be specific. Support each statement with examples, descriptions of projects or presentations, and/or quotations from the student's writing.

» Use carefully thought-out language, avoiding clichés, stock phrases, overgeneralizations, ambiguities, and exaggerations that may diminish your future credibility.

» If the student has received an honor or award in your subject area, explain the nature and significance of the award.

» Keep in mind the student's choice of school and academic program.

» Some very selective colleges ask you to compare the student you are writing about with other students whom you have recommended in the past. Consider limiting the number of recommendations to such a school to two or three per year. You might suggest to the student that another teacher write the recommendation if yours, under the conditions of comparison, will be less favorable.

THE COLLEGE INTERVIEW

Most students waste the interview—they don't prepare. They walk into my office and wait for something to happen. For these students, the interview is not a selection factor.
—Dean of Admissions, small public university

You need to learn how to use the interview to your advantage. The standard advice offered by well-intentioned people is "Be yourself," but that is much too general for gifted students; they think of too many alternatives. Gifted students may deal

To Whom It May Concern:

Sara is, without doubt, one of the most brilliant students I have ever had the pleasure of knowing. What is so extraordinary about her career here at Anderson High School is not just her distinguished performance, but her mastery of a challenging curriculum 2 years ahead of her classmates. Such precocity is uncommon in the field of English.

In the 2 years that I have taught her, Sara has demonstrated an intellectual maturity belying her age. As an 11th grader, when she was 15 years old, she excelled in my Advanced Placement (12th grade) English class for the gifted and talented. During that year her writing developed swiftly and consistently. Always one to seek the most difficult challenge, Sara wrote critical essays on works by authors such as William Faulkner and Thomas Mann with an understanding and expressiveness that touched the core of her subjects. Like a true writer, she drives herself, revising and polishing, always measuring her own achievement against that of the best writers—professional novelists, critics, and lately, poets. Sara frequently questions her own abilities, but, happily, this questioning leads her to new levels of artistic and intellectual activity. Her internal urge for perfection, her keen sense of form, and her unfailing imagination have enabled her to produce outstanding works in both literary analysis and fiction. Sara's short story, "The Tenth Tape," appeared in last year's literary arts magazine. One of my colleagues, having read the story, found it to be as absorbing as a "real story by an adult." It came as no surprise that Sara received the highest score (5) on the AP English examination.

This year Sara is my student in an independent study course, one that I designed especially for her as a sequel to the AP English course. It is exciting to participate in her continuous growth as an intellect and scholar. Thriving in an environment that allows her to set her own challenges, she pursues ideas with a rigor and scholarship that are enviable. In her most recent essay, on Virginia Woolf's *The Waves*, for example, she has presented a powerfully persuasive argument against critic James Naremore's contention

Figure 10. Sample teacher recommendation.

that the work is a failure, stifling in effect, and almost drowning the reader in language. Sara develops a countercriticism suggesting that, to the contrary, Woolf's language corresponds organically to the point she is making.

In my creative writing course, which Sara is taking as an elective, she seems to have discovered "her own voice." Her narratives, in unaffected, rhythmic prose, engage the reader and spark the imagination; her dialogues resonate with the natural sounds of speech. She can be intensely moving without any hint of sentimentality. Her artist's ear for sound and language has led her, perhaps inevitably, to write poetry. Sara's poems are impressive in their originality and craftsmanship. She has excellent control over rhythm and imagery, weaving lines like the following (from the middle of a surrealistic poem still in the draft stage):

> Mr. McGuire smiles at me/I see in his wide wet mouth/
> the spaces where his teeth once were/and try to run./
> My feet are caught in the vines, stuck/in thorny loops,
> and the cucumbers bulge/ like popping green fish-eyes/
> turning toward me in the wind . . . .

Despite the effort Sara puts into her creative and scholarly work, she still finds time to help others (she is the ideal student tutor: gentle, patient, and often funny) and to participate in extracurricular activities. She is an invaluable member of the English Team, the layout editor of the school newspaper, and the literary editor of the literary arts magazine, for which I am the adviser. We all enjoy working with Sara and know we can always count on her good judgment and imagination.

Sara is a wonderful combination of ingenuousness and brilliance. I admire her integrity, self-discipline, and generosity of spirit. She has my highest recommendation for admission to your university.

Signature
Title

Figure 10. Continued.

with general advice by focusing on one factor, such as how to dress for the interview, and then respond by swinging from one extreme to another. Some students will arrive in a sweatshirt and ragged jeans, others in a brand new suit or dress. In either case, you may be out of character and feel and look quite uncomfortable. Practice good eye contact and body language and a firm handshake.

Schools vary in whether they want to interview students and where they want to interview them. Use the school's website to find out how they set up an appointment.

Prior to an interview, you can review and discuss the list of questions presented later in this chapter. An interview practice session in which you and a classmate role-play an admissions officer and an applicant is an ideal way to demonstrate this part of the application process. You should decide which questions are important; however, you should be aware that highly selective colleges value certain questions. The factors that are important to you will determine the degree to which the college interview provides information that results in a match. For example, you may ask, "What are the most recent experiences your college has had in placing graduates in jobs, professional schools, or graduate schools?" If an admissions officer values that type of question and provides an adequate answer (one that goes beyond information provided in the guides), you will acquire valuable information and the admissions officer will have insight into what you want from a college.

Students, you should check to see whether on-campus interviews are offered. Many colleges now ask local alumni to conduct interviews; in this case, the local interviewer will contact you after your application is received.

Guidelines for an effective interview are presented shortly, but you should never "program" yourself to ask specific questions or answer questions in a specific way. Admissions officers recognize and value spontaneity. Consider, for example, the following two actual cases. Keep in mind that without strong academic credentials, neither of these candidates would be offered admission at a top tier university.

> During an interview, Kara noticed that her interviewer had a partially completed crossword puzzle on her desk. Kara mentioned the puzzle, and a conversation about their shared passion for puzzles followed. Kara recommended that the admissions officer subscribe to *Games* magazine. When she returned home, Kara wrote a thank-you note to the admissions officer, asking whether she had sent in a subscription to *Games* magazine.
>
> Following an interview during which it snowed heavily, Terrance found that his car was snowed in and immovable. He returned to the admissions office, where he and the admissions officer had a brief, humorous discussion about unexpected snowfalls. Terrance and the admissions officer solved the problem by convincing a campus security officer to help get the car to a relatively passable road. Following the interview he wrote a thank-you note to the admissions officer and added that he now carried a shovel and sand in his car to help him get out of snowdrifts.

Most of the suggestions listed in the guidelines that follow are general in nature. However, groups of students can rehearse scenarios in which the principles for specific colleges are followed. Guidelines for an effective interview include:

» Approach the interview with this in mind: You are about to invest thousands of dollars and 4 years of your life in an institution that may shape your values and career plans. What can you do during an interview to help you make the best decision about that investment and your future? If you do decide to invest in that institution, what information can you provide that will convince them to accept your application?

» If you are really interested in a selective college, research the institution thoroughly. Approach the interview as an opportunity to share information. Be prepared to say that you are interested and give reasons.

» Construct an agenda that asks questions that cannot be answered by reading college catalogs. For example, ask what percentage of the freshman class returns for sophomore year, or, if many students do not return, ask whether the college knows why. Do not ask how many books are in the library. There are more than you can read.

» Construct an agenda that will answer the personal question "What does this institution offer that will help me reach my goals?"

» Answer the interviewer's questions honestly. Prepare and rehearse, but don't overprogram yourself.

» Be prepared to present information about yourself that is not visible in your written application and supporting material. Open the conversation by stating your name and where you live, then offer your resume. Remember, the admissions committee is struggling to decide, "Which of these highly qualified applicants shall we admit, and which must we deny?" They probably have seen your application but not your resume. Presenting your resume avoids the age-old problem of what to say when your interviewer says, "Tell me something about yourself."

» Write down your interviewer's name; write a thank-you note as soon as you return home.

Remember, the interview is a time for colleges to provide information and evaluate you. An evaluative interview helps them determine whether you may be a better candidate than someone else for their school. An informational interview could be recruitment if a school already knows they want you. Schools vary in the importance they place on the interview; large public universities rarely offer interviews. However, if you are asked, take advantage of the opportunity. If they invite you to a Skype interview, take advantage of it. Some questions you may be asked in the interview include the following:

» Why do you want to go to this college?
» What do you want to know about this college?
» What have you read lately?
» Are there any particular subjects or authors you enjoy?
» How did you spend last summer?
» What has been important to you in high school?
» What do you consider to be your major strength? Weakness?
» Do you know what area you want to concentrate on in college? Why did you choose this particular area?
» During your free time at this school, in what activities might you participate?

Asking questions of the school representative during the interview may help you make your decision about whether or not you want to attend that college. Some questions you may want to ask during the interview include:

» What do you consider to be your outstanding departments?
» Can you take courses for credit in areas such as music and art if you are not going to major in them?
» At a university with a graduate school, you might want to ask: If I were in a preprofessional program here at your school, would it improve my chances of being admitted to your graduate school?
» Are there any opportunities to work on campus?
» Do you have an honor system (for student conduct and issues such as cheating) here? Are faculty members and students satisfied that everyone respects the honor system, especially during final examinations?

Relax and enjoy the conversation.

THE COLLEGE APPLICATION ESSAY

The essay is the bane of every high school senior's college application. Some students refuse to consider colleges where they might be extremely happy because an essay is required. Some students write their essays the night before the deadline; others spend weeks writing and rewriting. Only the college application deadline puts an end to the agony. If you have prior experience in writing, you will find that writing an autobiographical essay is a reflective, growth-promoting experience—after you overcome the anxiety produced by a series of open-ended, sometimes deceptively challenging questions such as "Tell us something about yourself that is not reflected in your application folder" or "Discuss your academic and professional goals."

You may have earned straight As in a highly rigorous academic program, earned more than adequate SAT or ACT scores, and have a social conscience and participate in many community activities, but still feel uneasy at the thought of outlining your academic and professional goals. How do you "evaluate a personal or educational experience" that has been "a major factor" in your getting old enough to apply to college? Given the age of most high school seniors, it is not surprising that some feel uncomfortable. You may wonder, "What does this question have to do with my ability to succeed in and contribute to that school?" The more competitive colleges, however, require essays, detailed written analyses of extracurricular activities, and/or personal statements. They are asking the question, "Who are you?" You should answer all questions, but in particular you should focus on the one that reads "What can you tell us about yourself that we have not asked?" If you take the time to write an effective answer to such a question, it may make the difference between acceptance and rejection.

Personal essays and statements should answer the question "Who are you?" from your perspective. The essay is your oppor-

168

tunity to take control. Questions reflect the college; responses reflect the student. Essays should answer the question that was asked and say something about your ability to organize, reflect, and write clearly. A well-written essay can make an applicant come alive on paper so that the reader can recognize him or her as a match for the college. If the essay is to make a significant difference to an admissions officer, you need to be aware of your strengths and limitations, and write reflectively.

The essay can be a decisive factor. It can reassure the admissions committee that you are capable of college-level work. Of course, admissions staff members read essays differently—we all have our own reading style—but in general, they are looking for qualities they believe are important. What are they looking for? Colleges look for the ability to use standard written English; content, substance, and depth of insight; and creativity and originality (see Figure 11). They also look for evidence of writing ability, intellectual curiosity, initiative and motivation, self-discipline, character, capacity for growth, leadership potential, and community service. They don't expect to find all of those attributes in one applicant, but they do expect to see consistency with other elements of your application. For example, if you claim to have strong leadership skills but do not hold a leadership position in any activities, that shows an inconsistency between your essay and your application.

The following prompts are several essay questions that you might see on a college application.

> » Students are asked to deal with a 2" x 4" rectangle on a blank piece of paper. The directions say, "Do something creative in this space. We are interested not only in your academic credentials, but also in your imagination and creativity."

> » You have just completed a 300-page autobiography. Please submit page 261.

> » You are a journalist with the rare opportunity to interview any person—living, deceased, or fictional. Whom would you choose? What do you feel you could learn from this person? Answer in 300 to 500 words.

169

☐	Writing ability	☐	Capacity for growth
☐	Intellectual curiosity	☐	Leadership potential
☐	Initiative and motivation	☐	Community service
☐	Creativity	☐	Consistency with other elements of the student's application
☐	Self-discipline		
☐	Character		

Figure 11. What colleges look for in admissions essays.

» Describe an experience that has altered or profoundly affected your present life or intended goals. The experience may be an accident, a competition, or anything of great significance to you.

» Make up a question, state it clearly, and answer it.

The above prompts represent three types of essays: "Tell Us About Yourself," "Why Us," and "Be Creative" (Springer et al., 2013).

Guidelines for Writing a College Application Essay

When there are no prompts or questions to answer, the following step-by-step process may help you practice and produce a better essay or personal statement.

1. Write several short essays. Write about what you do in school and what you do outside of school. (If you are an 11th-grade student, consider keeping a journal so that you will have many writing samples by application time.) Be specific. Be introspective. Look inside of yourself; don't just say what you think the school wants to hear. Avoid flattery. For example, you might write about:
   - your most important learning experience,
   - your favorite academic class or teacher,
   - the rise and fall of your science fair project,

- the trials and rewards of your work on a school publication,
- your selection as captain of the football team,
- your lack of athletic prowess,
- your work as a clerk at a discount store,
- your experience in a fast-food emporium, or
- a volunteer experience.

Here's an example. ACT uses the following prompt in its writing sample: Describe an issue relevant to high school students; ask examinees to write about their perspective on the issue.

2. Try to write about yourself in at least three different settings so that you can see yourself from several angles. List all of the adjectives you would use to describe yourself in each of these settings.

3. Define your characteristics. Ask yourself:
   - What outstanding characteristic or cluster of characteristics crop up in my writings?
   - Am I dependable, with good work habits?
   - Am I creative, with a good sense of humor?
   - Am I a person of contradictions? (Many of us are.)

4. Examine the question you are expected to answer.
   - Decide exactly what the question asks. You may want to check with your family or counselor; misinterpreting the question is a common mistake.
   - Decide which characteristics should be included in your answer.
   - Decide which example or examples should be included in your answer.

5. Write your answer.

6. Examine your answer. Try answering the following questions:

- Did my essay really answer the question? Am I the only person who could have written this essay? (If the answer is no, you need to examine ways to make your essay more reflective of you.)
- Does this essay include concrete examples to illustrate my points? (If the answer is no, you need to examine ways to include specific examples and illustrations.)
- Is this essay an interesting enough answer to the question that a reader will be able to concentrate on it after reading many other essays? (If the answer is no, you need to examine ways to help the reader remain interested.) Caution: Make your essay interesting, as opposed to strange and bizarre. For example, change the pacing and relate abstract concepts to concrete examples.

7. Revise your answer. Rewrite, rewrite, rewrite. You may need several revisions before you have an interesting essay that uses concrete examples and is self-reflective.
8. Edit your answer, checking grammar, spelling, and punctuation.
9. Type your essay. You do not want a tired admissions officer to attempt to read your handwriting at midnight after she has read hundreds of essays.
10. Mail your application.
11. Permit yourself one long sigh of relief!

Sample Student Essays

Essay questions vary from school to school and year to year. Highly selective schools generally phrase essay questions to encourage an applicant to write autobiographically—to describe something about himself that is not obvious in the application and supporting material.

The following samples were written by applicants to highly selective or selective universities in response to some general questions. Notice that they answer the question, as well as identify the student as both a problem finder and a problem solver.

Q: *What can you tell us about yourself that is not revealed in your application?*

A: *Student answer*

What is God?
Is He mod?
Is He of the old sod?
Does He have a bod?
Is He British or bluish or Jewish
Or Venusian?
Excuse-He-can all my sins.
Is He big-time on cloud nine or bovine
Or from Constantinople?
I-hope-He'll still let me in.
Hey, what's that storm brewing?
Doesn't He like what I'm doing?
What fate does He have stewing?
Is that lightning?
Oh crap.
Zap!

Slumping Senior
I am the slumping senior, I'm here to sing my song.
I've worked real hard the past 12 years but I've been in school
    too long.
I don't want all the pressure, but I know it's just begun.
If I had my way I'd skip every day,
I'd sleep till 10 and then be with my friends
And we could all go have some fun.
I am the slumping senior, I'm way too far behind.
If I get one more assignment, I think I'll lose my mind.
I've got an English paper, I've got a physics test;
I know it's true, tomorrow they're due,

I know it's late, if I start at eight
By four I'll get some rest.
I am the slumping senior, I've thought the whole thing
    through.
School won't really matter much when I'm 32.
I've learned to play the game of life, I think I'm doing fine
'Cause all the trends and all my friends
Are the only things worth remembering
When it's 10 years down the line.

I consider myself to be a "math" person. Problem solving in mathematics requires the application of definite processes to determine an answer that is either correct or incorrect. English is completely different; however, poetry provides a middle ground, which I thoroughly enjoy. Rhyme and rhythm give a poem a set pattern that I can follow easily, and the change of just one word can make the poem "correct" or "incorrect." My poems are always humorous, but vary from the outrageous "What is God?" to the autobiographical "Slumping Senior."

Q: *What activity have you participated in that has influenced you the most?*

A: *Student answer*

In the summer of _____, I had an experience that taught me more about myself than any other event in my life. I participated in a 3-week, multielement Outward Bound course in North Carolina consisting of rock climbing, canoeing, and hiking. Throughout the course I learned the importance of teamwork, commitment to achieving my goals, and the qualities of leadership. I will always reflect back on that unique experience as a time in my life when I learned so much that shaped my values, attitudes, and personality.

The most memorable experience I had there was rock climbing. I had never been so scared before in my life. Hundreds of feet up in the air, I held onto the face of a cliff by a metal clasp. Once I overcame my fear of falling I had to concentrate on climbing up the face. Many times I came to a dead end; I didn't quit, but only after I gained some confidence in myself would I find safety at the next ledge. From this experience I learned to trust myself and push the limit of my abilities. When I get stuck on something, I know I will keep trying new ways until I come up with the one that works for me. I believe that this lesson I learned will help me accomplish difficult tasks in college. I will not give up when things get tough because I know how it feels to achieve something for which I have struggled.

I learned teamwork in the canoeing part of the course. When two people are in a canoe together, it is crucial that they work together if they want to accomplish anything. I learned this lesson the hard way. Only after smashing into submerged boulders and capsizing into roaring rapids did I realize that I couldn't do everything on my own. This lesson of teamwork will help me in college, where I know that I will have to work with faculty and other students to get the best possible education.

Another experience I had of pushing my limits was the last event of the course, a 14-mile marathon. The choice was given to us to run nine or 14 miles. I chose the 14 miles because I didn't know if I could do it or not and I wanted to know what my limits were. It felt so good to finish that race, knowing that I accomplished something that I hadn't known if I could do. I find it amazing how people can always perform past what they believe to be their limits. I will always remember this experience because whenever I come to a problem in my life I know I won't take the easy way out.

The most grueling part of the course was hiking. We had to carry all our food, equipment, and clothes in our packs and hike up and down hills for long periods of time without rest. Through this part of the course I learned that I do have leadership qualities. I put a lot of effort into finding trails, organizing campsites, and taking charge of expeditions. On one occasion, when we had lost the trail and the rest of the group had given up, I made a very determined effort to find the trail and led the group to our destination. From this experience I found that I don't like to sit back and let other people do things for me. I like to make things happen for myself, to create opportunities. This enthusiasm and creativity will help me excel in college.

These experiences will always be memorable to me because they have helped me discover what kind of person I am. The values and attitudes I have developed from these experiences will help me with my future in college and in my life.

Q: *In an essay of no more than 300 words, explain how you feel that engineering and applied science can best benefit humanity in the next decade.*

A: *Student Answer*

The science of engineering always involves the recognition of a problem and the determination to solve it. The size of the problem is irrelevant. It can vary from something as small as the configuration of a paper clip to something as large as putting a man on the moon. The method of solving the problem is the same. It involves proposing possible solutions within a set scientific procedure.

Engineering is an integral part of human progress. Without it there would be no answers or solutions to the challenges man has faced through the centuries. It is easy to see how far mankind has come and, at the same time, to see that we have just begun to develop. I think the next decade will involve the need for thinkers and planners trained in engineering. We are on the verge of discovering many exciting solutions, including the cures for many diseases and the establishment of a space station. Discoveries in space for aerospace engineers are just as important as a cure for cancer is for the biomedical engineer. Some may think the latter is more important. It may be, but the dreams of the engineers and the challenges they face in finding solutions are the same. That is the important part. It is hard to predict the future and to know what particular discovery will be more beneficial than another, but one thing is clear: without a group of well-trained engineers, those discoveries won't be made.

It can be said that engineering is one of the oldest professions. It hasn't always been called engineering, of course, but there have always been people who have looked for answers within an engineering framework. That is how man has progressed scientifically. As we head into the next century, engineers will be ready to raise questions and propose solutions.

TIPPING THE BALANCE

Each year, colleges have to select their freshman class from a host of qualified students. It is important to look at some of the more subtle factors that are considered and that can tip the balance in favor of admission when a college is making up the freshman class.

» What does the school need, and are you uniquely qualified to fill that need? Special or unique qualities that you will bring to a college community can tip the balance your favor.

» Would you contribute diversity to the campus? Although colleges are not permitted to decide admissions solely on the basis of race or culture, campus diversity is highly valued. Your ethnic origins may tip the balance in your favor.

» Are you a legacy or does your family have an educational history at this school? A legacy means "something handed down." In the case of college admissions, it literally means that admission is handed down from the parent alumnus. If either of your parents attended a university where you have applied, that makes you a legacy. If you do not have the academic record required by that college, it won't make a difference. But in a tough competition where you need an edge, being a legacy can tip the balance in your favor.

Decisions: The College Envelope Arrives, Now What?

If your application for admission has been accepted by more than one school—and if you followed the process outlined in this book and chose wisely, that will surely happen—how are you going to decide which college you should attend?

» Revisit the schools that seriously interest you. Colleges often look different than they did when you were "just looking." Try to arrange an overnight stay in the dorms, sit in on a freshman class, eat several meals, and visit the library.

» Look again at what you wanted from a school when you used the questionnaire in this book. Is that fascinating professor going to teach freshmen, or do teaching assistants teach his or her classes? Are the professors friendly?

» Check out college nightlife. Nightlife may seem like a trivial consideration, but it's hard to spend 4 years accomplishing your academic goals if you hate your life because there's nothing to do. Having fun is one of the keys to staying sane.

» Talk to people. If an alumnus interviewed you, talk to that person about campus life. Talk to students. Go to the website and see if there are blogs that will give you a sense of what it's like to be a student at that school.

» Do not "double-deposit"—that is, send deposits to more than one school. It's unethical.

Waiting Lists

If enough accepted students enroll for freshman year, the college won't accept anyone from the wait list. Colleges pride themselves on accurately predicting their "yield" (that is, the percentage of admitted students who will actually enroll). Their financial stability depends on full classrooms and full dorm rooms.

A NACAC (2012) Admission Trend survey of its members indicated that between 2007 and 2010, colleges with wait lists admitted fewer than one third of wait listed students. Because not all colleges are members of NACAC, the adjusted norm for all colleges was more like 10%.

The most selective colleges and universities placed a larger proportion of total applicants on the wait list, admitted a smaller percentage of wait listed students, and a higher percentage of students accepted from the wait list actually enrolled. More than 80% of colleges that maintain wait lists provide written information about their wait list policies to students. Common features of written information pertaining to wait list policies include directions for remaining on the wait list (93%), the amount of time students have to respond to being accepted from the wait list (64%), and the last date that admission offers will be made (59%). Over half (53%) of wait list institutions did use a phone call to notify students of acceptance from the wait list.

In 2004, 57% of all wait-listed students opted to remain on the wait list. An average of 27% of all students who were placed on the wait list ultimately gained admission to the college or university that wait-listed them (NACAC, 2004a). As you can see, these percentages have not changed very much. Over half of the colleges surveyed ultimately enrolled 30% of the students who were originally placed on the wait list.

What happens if you are placed on the waiting list of a school you really want to attend? There are several things you can do.

» First, ensure your place at a school that accepted your application by sending a deposit.

» Plan a new strategy. Write a letter to the college that wait-listed you and ask to remain active on their wait list, assuming that school is your first choice. You are, in effect, telling them that if you are offered admission, you will accept. However, colleges may not request a deposit prior to offering admission (NACAC Principles of Good Practice, 2013).

» Find out what being on the waiting list means at the particular college. That is, ask how many students they usually accept from the waiting list, and if they rank students on the waiting list. According to the NACAC (Gross, 2002), about one third of colleges and universities use wait lists, and a student's chances of admission is about one in five. These are general numbers and subject to change each year because the wait list is not actually a ranked list. In some cases it might be a table of sticky notes just waiting for something to happen. That something might be a convincing letter from a guidance counselor or some important credentials that fell out.

» Ask your guidance counselor to find out why you were placed on the waiting list. The reasons will help determine the best action to take. For example, if your folder indicates specific weaknesses, you may be able to submit substantive additional information that will influence the dean or director of admissions.

» If the college considers you a "viable" candidate, or one who will be accepted if a vacancy develops, ask your guidance counselor to lobby actively for you.

» If one or more of your teacher recommendations is less than laudatory, you may want to find additional recommendations and ask to see them before they are sent.

» Write or fax to the dean of admissions, telling him or her that you were waitlisted, and indicating that you want to attend the school if there is a vacancy. Ask him or her to review your folder. State your reasons for requesting that your application be reviewed.

» Find out the projected schedule for admitting students on the waiting list. Ask when you can expect to hear from the college. It may happen as soon as June or as late as August, so you have to decide how badly you want to attend that school.

» Apply elsewhere. Some colleges have nontraditional admission. That is, they admit students during the winter break before the second semester. Or, you might enter a school on probation, in which case it's up to you to prove you can do the work.

» Consider attending your second-choice college or university for a year. You may have a better chance as a transfer applicant than as a graduating high school senior, if you can prove that you are capable of high achievement.

What if you are rejected by all of the colleges you applied to? Do not despair. Ask your guidance counselor to find out the reason for each rejection. Compare the reasons. Is there a pattern or central theme? The answers to some of the following questions will determine your action:

» Were *all* of the schools flooded with applicants this year?
» Was there some confusion regarding the presentation of information in your application?
» Did you have a specific academic weakness?

If there is no central theme, perhaps you miscalculated your options. For example, did you apply to a range of schools that included at least one that you knew would accept your application and several whose admission requirements matched your credentials? After May 1, NACAC maintains a list of colleges that still have openings. Your counselor can help you decide on which of these colleges you should apply to. You will find additional helpful tips on the NACAC website in their online booklet, "Guide to the College Admission Process" (http://www.nacacnet.org/research/PublicationsResources/Marketplace/Documents/GCAP2011_Web.pdf).

The following are some possibilities for strengthening your chances at a later time:

» Look at other colleges with similar characteristics.
» Submit additional applications to colleges with rolling or late admissions policies.
» After June 1, inquire about unanticipated openings. (This is called "summer meltdown.")

» Spend a year investigating career paths: Find an internship, work in a law office, or volunteer for a community service project.
» Spend a year bolstering your academic weaknesses: Take some courses at a local community college to prove you can do college-level work.
» Look for a sense of direction and begin again!

COLLEGE COSTS

This section is a general overview of college costs to help families be more resourceful. However, college cost information changes yearly. For current detailed information, consult the publications *The A's and B's of Academic Scholarships* (Leider, 2011), *College.edu* (Guernsey, 2011), and *Don't Miss Out: The Ambitious Student's Guide to Financial Aid* (Leider & Leider, 2011). More information about college costs is available online at http://www.finaid.org and http://www.thinktuition.com.

The Bad News

Educating a gifted student after high school is not a one-shot, one-year affair. Gifted students often invest heavily in both time and money in post-high-school education. Think of it in terms of 2 years for an associate degree, 4 years for a bachelor's, 6 years or longer for a graduate or professional degree, and even longer if there are younger brothers or sisters spaced 2 or 4 years apart. You and your family may pay college bills for many years following high school graduation, so it is important to understand the overall costs of college.

What stands out immediately is cause for concern. Each year the cost of a college education and our ability to pay it are reassessed by a federally approved system called *need analysis*. If current trends continue, costs will continue to outpace inflation. If tuition increases at twice the estimated inflation rate (hypothetically 3.2%), a $12,000 tuition bill in a student's freshman year will be a $20,000 tuition bill 4 years later. At this writing, 58 colleges have passed the $50,000 (annually) mark for tuition, fees, and room and board. In addition, the interest rates on student loans continue to increase. And approximately half of those who enter college do not finish (Selingo, 2013).

There are several reasons why tuition and other college costs continue to rise. First, higher education is labor intensive. Great teaching comes from conversation and discussion among inquiring minds. But, faculty salaries are comparatively low, so catch-up raises are necessary to attract new professors and keep tenured faculty members from leaving academia for higher incomes in the corporate world.

Second, state support for higher education is lagging behind increased cost. Public universities, as well as community colleges, depend on state appropriations for more than half their support. When appropriations fail to match rising costs, colleges must compensate by raising in-state tuition and sharply raising tuition for out-of-state students.

The third factor is technology. To provide high-quality education, colleges need to spend money for up-to-date laboratories, research equipment, and wireless campuses, as well as the supporting maintenance and training staffs.

Finally, with few exceptions, colleges can no longer meet the financial needs of all students. One solution is to raise tuition rates by two to three times the rate of inflation. Students who can afford the increases are, in effect, helping to subsidize those who need financial aid.

In addition to the news that tuition will continue to outpace inflation, a second bit of bad news is that federal student aid continues in a lean cycle. Although the dollar amount of federal grants and loans increases each school year, new programs are being added and other programs are being stretched to help reduce the federal budget deficit.

Of equal concern is the unstable delivery of federal student aid. In order to add, cut, or stretch some programs, the associated timetables, eligibility rules, interest rates, and even student aid forms have changed from year to year. These changes will continue in magnitude and frequency. The result is confused students, parents, and guidance counselors and extremely overworked college financial aid personnel.

The Good News

Most colleges must compete for good students. This competition for the right student translates into recruiting drives, alumni interviews, special honors programs, and scholarships designed to attract the brightest available students. The more marketable the student—good IB/ACT/SAT scores, grade point average, and class standing, together with leadership, athletic ability, or talent—the more nonfederal, college-sponsored student financial assistance there is to help defray college costs.

Additional good news for students from low-income families is that "a handful of schools have instituted policies that ensure that low income students have no loans in their financial aid packages" (FinAid.org, n.d., para. 1). If your family's yearly income is below a certain level—about $40,000 or $60,000, depending on the school—there are a number of schools that will meet the student's full financial need through grants or a combination of grants and work-study programs, rather than requiring students to take out loans that they will later have to repay. For a list of schools with such policies, see http://www.finaid.org/questions/noloansforlowincome.phtml.

Getting Your Fair Share

Before you reach for a share of these extra dollars, you need to understand what makes up the student's part of college costs, namely the cost of attendance. The cost of attendance consists of six separate items: tuition, room, board, books, transportation, and miscellaneous expenses. Miscellaneous expenses include insurance and laundry costs, and the cost of eating at restaurants and other forms of recreation.

The cost of attendance is different for each student, even for students at the same college. Some students live in dormitories, others in off-campus housing, and others at home with their parents. The cost of travel or commuting varies depending upon circumstances.

The most expensive private college in the United States costs more than $60,000 per year for tuition, room, and board. The cost of 4 years at an Ivy-League school could be as high as $240,000. Depending on whether you are an in-state or out-of-state student, 4 years at a public institution can range from $48,000 to $120,000.

A student can normally receive assistance in meeting college costs if the calculated *family contribution* is lower than the cost of attending the school. The difference between the two is the *financial need*.

Having financial need means you may qualify for student aid in order to attend the college of your choice. For example, Alex's family is able to contribute $12,000 per year to his college costs. He is considering three universities: Ivy X, at about $45,000 per year; Midrange U, at about $33,000; and Home State U, which will cost about $12,000. Alex's family has calculated their financial need and the amount they would qualify for in student aid. At Ivy X they would qualify for $35,000 to help with the annual cost, at Midrange U they would qualify for $21,000 in aid, and at Home State U there would be no financial need at all.

Understanding Family Contributions

The amount of money a family is able to contribute to college costs is the key to estimating the amount of financial aid for which they will qualify. The family contribution is essentially the sum of four separate calculations: the contribution from the parents' income, the contribution from the parents' assets, the contribution from the student's income, and the contribution from the student's assets (Berkner, Berker, Rooney, & Peter, 2003; Wei et al., 2009).

Parental income includes the total of all taxable and nontaxable income. A family maintenance allowance is subtracted from this total. The larger the family, the larger the allowance. Income and social security taxes are also subtracted. The remainder is referred to as discretionary income. Depending on the amount, a percentage is taken and the result is considered the parents' contribution from income.

The next calculation is a percentage of the value of the parents' assets. The total value of savings, stocks, bonds, trust funds, mutual funds, money market funds, commodities, land and mortgage contracts held, and business and farm assets is calculated when considering eligibility for federal assistance. An asset protection allowance for retirement is subtracted based on the age of the oldest parent. Approximately 5.6% of the remainder is added to the family contribution. You can expect a private institution to add home equity to the list before they will use any of their scarce resources to assist a student.

Next, the student receives a $5,250 after-tax income protection allowance. Fifty percent of income over the allowance is added to the family contribution. Finally, the student's assets are evaluated. No asset protection allowance is permitted, because the student is considered to have a full working life ahead of him or her. The formula adds 20% of the student's assets to the family contribution (Berkner et al., 2003).

The sum of these four calculations, the family contribution to college cost, is what the student is expected to pay for his or her college education. The family contribution subtracted from the cost for a particular college determines the amount of student financial need and the amount of student aid for the school year. The calculation is recomputed each school year.

Multistudent Families. What happens if there is more than one member of a family in college at the same time? How does the family contribution to college cost change? In this common situation, a separate family contribution is calculated for each student, con-

186

sisting of the parents' contribution from income and assets. For example, suppose that the total parental contribution is $12,000 and there are two students. Then $6,000 is allocated to each student. Son Jason's contribution from earnings and assets is $1,500, while daughter Gina's is $2,000. Consequently, the family contribution for Jason's college cost will be $7,500, and for Gina's will be $8,000.

Divorced or Separated Parents. Which parent's income and assets are used in the calculation when parents are divorced or separated? The answer depends upon which parent the student lived with for the greater portion of the calendar year preceding the year the student enters college. If the custodial parent has remarried, stepparent income and assets are included. Also, a student facing this situation and seeking nonfederal college financial assistance should be aware that most private colleges will likely ask the other natural parent to submit a divorced-parent financial form before awarding any financial assistance.

Filling Out the Forms

How do colleges get the information they need to calculate the family contribution to college cost? As soon as possible after the first of the year, the student and his or her family should fill out a need-analysis form called the Free Application for Federal Student Aid (FAFSA). Students applying for early selection must do this twice, first when they apply, and again after the first of the year.

A student seeking to determine whether he or she qualifies for some of the college's own money or money from the state in which the student resides in addition to federal financial aid, may be required to fill out the College Board's CSS Profile or the American College Testing Program's family financial statement. Both forms require a processing fee. Information about these forms is normally obtained from high school guidance offices and college financial aid offices. Some colleges have unique financial aid forms attached to the admission application.

Putting Scholarships to Work

Most people believe that receipt of a scholarship reduces their family contribution to college costs. However, while the scholarship will help pay the college bill, it may not reduce the student's or the family's share of the bill.

For example, the Johnson family contribution was determined to be $9,000. At her high school commencement, her town civic association awarded Sally Johnson a $1,000 scholarship. The Johnsons were elated, thinking that their family contribution would now be $8,000. Unfortunately, they were wrong: The contribution remained the same. By law, Sally's college just took the amount of the scholarship and incorporated it into Sally's student aid package.

This does not mean that students heading for college should stop looking for and working toward scholarships and grants. Rather, they should concentrate their efforts on seeking scholarships large enough to cover both the family contribution and the student aid award. The best advice is not to waste time seeking special scholarships or seeking out computerized scholarship services that charge a fee for their work. Saving money for college is a better course of action. Some scholarship money goes unused each year, but it is primarily unused employee tuition benefits, not scholarships for which no one has applied.

Financial Aid in Return for Service in the Military or Other Government Programs

Persons serving in all branches of the U.S. Armed Forces on active duty or in the Reserves, or those participating in a Reserve Officer Training Corps (R.O.T.C.) program while attending college, can earn entitlements that may cover up to 100% of college tuition, fees, and books, plus additional dollars for expenses. In addition, a variety of federal government programs such as AmeriCorps and others at the state level offer funds for college tuition for those who volunteer and complete their terms of service.

More About Money

According to the US Department of Education, in the 2009–2010 academic year, the latest year for which statistics are available, more than 20 million undergraduates were enrolled in postsecondary institutions for all or part of the year as full- or part-time students, in both public and private colleges (U.S. Department of Education, 2011). Forty-seven percent of all undergraduates received federal student aid in 2007–2008, the average amount of which was $6,600. In 2007–2008, federal Pell Grants were awarded to 27% of all undergraduates at an average of $2,600, and 34% of all undergraduates took out federal Stafford loans averaging a total of $5,000. Subsidized Stafford loans were received by 30% of undergraduates and averaged $3,400, while 22% received an average of $3,200 in unsubsidized Stafford loans (Wei et al., 2009). It's quite likely that when temporary funding runs out, the Pell Grant program will be cut by half, so if you are looking for grant money, make sure you are looking at the latest figures, usually on the Department of Education website.

According to the College Board (n.d.c), the average comprehensive tuition rate for public ($11,376) and private colleges ($27,485) is significantly higher than the mean federal grant disbursed per student. On average, the institutions with the highest tuition are private institutions with small enrollments, institutions that are highly selective, and those that have low yield rates. Private colleges and colleges with low enrollments also have a slightly larger percentage of students receiving federal grant aid than public schools and those with high enrollments. Dependent need-based aid is provided to students based on their family income and their need for financial assistance. Non-need-based state aid, including merit aid, has continued to grow over the last 10 years. Non-need-based aid is awarded to students based on factors not pertaining to income, such as high academic achievement. Currently, 77% of state financial aid is distributed through need-based aid, and 23% through non-need-based aid (Leider, 2011; Leider & Leider, 2011).

Next to buying a home and paying for retirement, the cost of sending children to college is the largest financial challenge most parents face. If you wait until your children are in high school before saving, when your child graduates from high school you probably won't have enough to pay for 4 years of college. So, do some research, start saving early, and be consistent in depositing money into whatever type of account you choose. Here are five ways to save money for college (Willis, 2005):

1. Coverdell Education Savings Account (ESA) plans are similar to Individual Retirement Accounts (IRA) in that they are tax-sheltered investment accounts available to U.S. taxpayers who deposit up to a maximum of $2,000 per year that will be used for college (Savingforcollege. com, n.d.a). Savings are tax deferred. If more than one person is depositing to a child's account, care must be taken that the total does not exceed the limit—$2,000. If the contribution is not used for education, eventually the funds will revert back to the student. You can't just refund the account back to yourself.

2. 529 accounts are education savings plans operated by a state or educational institution designed to help families set aside funds for future college costs. The plans are named after Section 529 of the Internal Revenue Code. There are 92 separate state 529 plans that vary widely and there are some national plans for those who move frequently. There is no annual contribution limit, as there is with the ESA. Savings are tax-deferred for a limited number of years (Savingforcollege.com, n.d.b). These plans may be accompanied by hefty fees, so look carefully before you jump into one. Do your homework and talk to a financial planner to compare the plans and look at how well they perform over time. What happens if the 529 account beneficiary doesn't go to college? You can transfer the account to another college-bound beneficiary, as long as he or she is an eligible family member. If you don't use a 529 account for eligible expenses,

earnings on your withdrawals are taxable and usually subject to a penalty.

3. Prepaid state tuition plans allow you to save money by paying for college now, but only if your teen will attend a state school. It may sound good, but prepaid tuition plans reduce financial aid eligibility.

4. Education savings bonds are a risk-free investment, but there is a limit on exemptions if your adjusted gross income is too high. The money is held in the parent's name, which can be a good thing, because the child isn't penalized when applying for financial aid.

5. Large corporations like McDonald's or Staples, and more than 40,000 retail stores, 7,000 restaurants, 10,000 hotels, and 350 online retailers will give you college contributions through the Upromise rebate program (see http://www.upromise.com). The Upromise website describes the program as a "free rebating program that helps families save money for college." Major companies where you can get rebates include Macy's, Sears, Target, and Best Buy.

Some Final Words

The matter of paying college costs should not be taken lightly. A parent should not "let Johnny worry about it," any more than Johnny should "let Mom and Dad worry about it." The entire family needs to get involved.

Paying college costs requires research, study, and analysis. It should be discussed with high school counselors and college financial aid personnel, who have special knowledge of personal financial matters—loans, interest rates, tax laws, and innovative tuition payment plans. Knowing as much as possible about college costs can save time and money. What is most important is to know and understand the details about the entire spectrum of financing a gifted student's college education *before* filling out the first financial assistance form.

College Planning Glossary and Glossary of Financial Terms

Academic performance: the combination of a student's grade point average (GPA), class rank, transcript, standardized test scores, evidence of academic rigor, and other available numerical information. Some large schools consider a student's high school academic performance record the only criterion for an offer of admission.

Academic rigor: the relative difficulty of an academic course and the relative difficulty of all courses taken by a student during high school. Highly selective colleges expect a student to take the most rigorous curriculum offered.

Advanced Placement (AP) examinations: exams offered each May by participating schools to students who want to be tested at the college level in many areas, including English, calculus, science, foreign languages, and music. Enrollment in an AP course is not required, and a fee is charged for each examination. AP tests are scored 1 to 5, with 5 being the highest score. Grades of 3, 4, or 5 on AP examinations may be considered acceptable for college credit or exemption from required courses. Each college or university decides how much credit will be awarded to the student, and highly selective schools may give credit only for a 5. If a student takes an AP test, the student is responsible for ensuring that the score reaches the college.

Advanced Placement (AP) Program: program sponsored by the College Entrance Examination Board consisting of rigorous academic courses and examinations in 15 subjects. AP courses provide an opportunity for students to pursue college-level studies while still enrolled in secondary school, and demonstrate the student's capacity to handle college-level work. A high grade in an AP course is considered evidence of superior ability, even if a student doesn't take the AP test.

ACT assessment test: a content-oriented test, divided into four subject areas—math, science, English, and social studies—and an optional writing section. Scores are reported on a scale of 1 to 36, with 36 being the highest.

Class rank: computation denoting a student's academic position in relation to classmates. Class rank is generally reported in terms of deciles, quarters, and/or thirds. Grade point average usually determines class rank.

College: (1) a postsecondary school that offers a bachelor's degree in liberal arts, science, or both, and (2) schools of a university offering the aforementioned degree programs.

College cost calculator: By law, colleges are now required to provide a college cost calculator on their website so families can get an idea of their expected family contribution.

Federal work-study program: a federally financed program that provides opportunities for students who need financial aid to work on campus or with tax-exempt employers. Work-study programs should not be confused with cooperative education programs run by many colleges to provide students with practical work experience based on their particular college major.

Deferred admission: allows an accepted student to postpone admission to college for one year.

Early admission or early entrance: procedure that admits students of unusually high ability into college courses and programs before they have completed high school.

Early action (EA): procedure whereby students submit credentials to colleges early, usually by November 1. Unlike early decision, a student admitted under early action is not obligated to enroll.

Early decision (ED): procedure that gives special consideration to a student who applies for admission by a specified date. If admitted under early decision, the student has an obligation to attend that school. The student may not accept an offer of admission from another institution at a later date. Some schools have two rounds of early decision, ED 1 and ED 2. The date for ED 2 often coincides with regular admission decisions, but ED 2 students have priority. Schools take a fresh look at them before the regular admission students. A second round allows the school to receive applications from students who were not offered ED admission by their first choice school.

Expected family contribution: the amount that an accrediting agency estimates that a student's family should be able to contribute toward his or her education. The amount takes into account parent resources, the student's savings, the family's earnings, and the student's earnings.

Family financial statement: a financial aid application form required by colleges using the ACT assessment for admissions purposes.

Federal Stafford Loans: government subsidized and unsubsidized (you pay the interest), low-interest loans made to students by credit unions, commercial banks, or savings and loan institutions. Repayment of a subsidized loan is guaranteed by the federal government. The amount that students may borrow and the number of years they have to repay it vary from year to year.

Free Application for Federal Student Aid (FAFSA): government need-analysis form that determines the expected family contribution and Pell Grant eligibility. Watch out for deadlines, the regular deadline, and the deadline for corrections.

Grant: the portion of a financial aid package that the student does not have to repay.

Grade point average (GPA): number usually computed by giving quality points to each letter grade (for academic and nonacademic courses) earned during high school and then dividing by the number of earned credits. Some school systems "weigh" honors or Advanced Placement (AP) courses by awarding extra points or fractions of points for the courses. Colleges frequently recalculate a student's GPA to reflect only his or her academic courses.

High school profile, course description, or transcript supplement: provides information to colleges about the high school's program of studies, grading system, and makeup of the student body. The meaning of a student's transcript (grades) is partially explained by an effective profile that includes the percentage of students who go to 4-year colleges, the nature of the courses offered, and the grading scale. When a course title does not clearly reflect the rigor and significance of an academic course, an explanation should accompany the school profile and student transcript.

Liberal arts: academic disciplines such as language, history, literature, and philosophy. These programs are designed not to prepare a student for a profession but for the development of intellectual ability and judgment.

Merit-based awards and scholarships: scholarships awarded by colleges and outside agencies on the basis of student accomplishment, rather than financial need. Merit scholarships may be awarded on the basis of a student's PSAT scores and the results of the National Merit Scholarship competition. Some merit-based awards target students of different backgrounds, cultures, and races.

Massive Online Open Courses (MOOC): an online course aimed at large-scale interactive participation and open access via the web. In addition to traditional course materials such as videos, readings, and problem sets, MOOCs provide interactive user forums that help build a community for the students, professors, and teaching assistants (TAs). MOOCs are a recent development in distance education and have proved to be extremely popular.

Needs-based scholarships and awards: scholarships awarded on the basis of *demonstrated* financial need. You must submit personal family financial information to prove your need.

Official transcript: academic profile of the student. Transcripts should include a list of courses taken each year (including courses in progress), the rigor of those courses (AP, honors, accelerated), grades assigned for each course, GPA, and class rank (including how the rank is determined).

Parent loan for undergraduate students: primarily a loan for parents of dependent students. Loans are made directly to parents.

Pell Grants: grants given under a federal program for extremely needy families. Grants under this program ranged from $500 to $5,500 as of this writing. However, students will only be able to use them for 12 semesters instead of 18 semesters.

Perkins Loan: a low-interest loan for students with demonstrated need. Students do not apply directly for a Perkins Loan; funds are paid directly to colleges by the federal government for allocation to students whom the colleges select.

PIN: personal identification number used to complete the online FAFSA. Both student and parent must apply for a PIN.

Preliminary SAT®/National Merit Scholarship Qualifying Test (PSAT/NMSQT): a 2-hour version of the SAT. The PSAT is a screening mechanism for the National Merit Scholarship competition. In order to be considered, students must take the test in the fall of 11th grade and score in the top 5% of students in their state. The PSAT is similar to the SAT and is therefore a good preliminary indicator of the student's potential SAT score. PSAT scores are also used for the National Merit Hispanic Scholarship and the National Achievement Scholarship Program for Outstanding Negro Students.

Profile: designed by the college scholarship service for participating colleges and scholarship awarding foundations. You must register and complete this form online. Profile requires the same basic data as FAFSA, with extra questions about assets, expenses, and resources.

Quarter system: divides the 9-month academic year into three equal parts of approximately 12 weeks each. Summer sessions are usually the same length. Credits are granted as quarter hours (3 quarter hours = 2 semester hours).

Regular admission: admission to a college in the usual manner. Students must submit an application by a specified date, and a decision is made by the college after it has received most of its applications (approximately February 15 to April 15). All applicants are informed at about the same time, although this varies with the college.

Reserve Officers' Training Corps (ROTC): students take part in training for a career in the military; tuition, books, and fees are subsidized by the military, and the student also receives a stipend to help cover personal expenses. Upon graduation, students receive a commission in the military service. Students may be obligated to serve a specified number of years in the military after graduation.

Reserve Officers' Training Corps (ROTC) scholarship: a scholarship and educational program offered by the U.S. military. In return for scholarship aid, students are obligated to serve for a period of years on active duty or reserve status in one of the military services.

Rolling admission: admission to a college whereby students may submit an application at any time during the year. The college makes a decision within a few weeks of receiving the application and transcript.

SAT: a nearly 4-hour-long test divided into three sections: verbal, mathematics, and a writing exercise. Scores are reported on a scale of 200 to 800 in each section. A perfect score is 2400.

SAT or ACT preparatory courses: courses taken to prepare a student for the SAT or ACT tests.

SAT Subject Tests: one-hour tests similar to final examinations in a variety of academic subjects such as mathematics, science, history, language, literature, and writing. Subject tests are designed to measure the extent and depth of a student's knowledge of the subject.

Semester system: divides the academic year into two equal segments of approximately 18 weeks each. Summer sessions are shorter, but they require more intensive study.

Single choice early action (SCEA): also referred to as nonbinding early decision. Similar to early decision, if a student applies to a SCEA college, the student is prohibited from applying either early decision or early action to other colleges, but may apply regular admission anywhere else. Like early action, students are not bound to attend the SCEA college if they are accepted.

Student aid report: report indicates the expected family contribution and whether or not a student is eligible for a Pell Grant.

Supplemental educational opportunity grant: grant designed to provide additional support for Pell Grants based on student need. Money is paid directly to colleges to give to needy students.

Trimester system: divides the calendar year into three segments, thereby creating a continuous academic calendar of three semesters, each approximately 18 weeks in length. Credits are usually granted in semester hours.

University: a postsecondary school consisting of teaching and research facilities comprising a graduate school or professional schools. Universities offer master's degrees and doctorates, as well as undergraduate degrees.

REFERENCES

ACT Inc. (n.d.a). *Frequently asked questions about the ACT writing test.* Retrieved from http://www.act.org/aap/writing/highschool/faq.html#8

ACT Inc. (n.d.b). *The ACT writing test.* Retrieved from http://www.act.org/aap/writing/index.html

Abrams, T. (2013a, May 13). *Advice from a dean of admissions on selecting high school courses* [Web log post]. Retrieved from http://thechoice.blogs.nytimes.com/2013/05/13/selecting-high-school-courses/?_r=0

Abrams, T. (2013b, July 22). *7 of 8 Ivy League schools report lower acceptance rates* [Web log post]. Retrieved from http://thechoice.blogs.nytimes.com/2013/03/28/ivy-league-college-admission-rates-2013/

Adams, C. (2013, November 11). *Students' planned majors and academic interests are often out of sync* [Web log post]. Retrieved from http://blogs.edweek.org/edweek/college_bound/2013/11/high_school_students_planned_college_majors_and_academic_interests_often_are_a_mismatch.html

Americans with Disabilities Act, 42 U.S.C. §§ 12102 et seq. (1990).

Baum, S. (1990). *Gifted but learning disabled: A puzzling paradox.* Retrieved from ERIC database. (ED321484)

Baum, S., & Ma, J. (2013). *Trends in college pricing, 2013* (Trends in Higher Education Series). Retrieved from http://trends. collegeboard.org/sites/default/files/college-pricing-2013-full-report.pdf

Baum, S., & Payea, K. (2004). *Education pays: The benefits of higher education for individuals and society.* New York, NY: College Entrance Examination Board.

Berger, S. L. (2013). *The best summer programs for teens.* Waco, TX: Prufrock Press.

Berkner, L., Berker, A., Rooney, K., & Peter, K. (2003). *Student financing of undergraduate education: 1999–2000.* Retrieved from http://nces.ed.gov/programs/quarterly/vol_4/4_3/4_2. asp

Boyd, L. (1999). *I.B. or not I.B.? That is the question.* Retrieved from http://www.afsa.org/fsj/Dec99/boyd.cfm

Clinton, W. J. (1997). *Opening wide the doors of college. President Clinton's call to action for American education in the 21st century.* Retrieved from http://www.ed.gov/updates/PresEDPlan/ part9.html

Cohn, D. (2011). *Lifetime earnings of college graduates.* Retrieved from http://www.pewsocialtrends.org/2011/05/16/lifetime -earnings-of-college-graduates/

Cohn, D. (2013). *College-educated Americans take bigger share of the income pie.* Retrieved from http://www.pewsocialtrends. org/2013/09/24/college-educated-americans-take-bigger-share-of-the-income-pie/

College Board. (n.d.a). *Meet the SAT: What it means to your child.* Retrieved from http://www.collegeboard.com/parents/arti cle/0,3708,700-702-0-21295,00.html

College Board. (n.d.b). *SAT reasoning test.* Retrieved from http:// www.collegeboard.com/student/testing/sat/about/SATI. html

College Board. (n.d.c). *Trends in college pricing, 2005.* Retrieved from http://www.collegeboard.com/prod_downloads/press/cost05/trends_college_pricing_05.pdf

College Board. (2013). *Annual AP Program participation 1956–2013.* Retrieved from http://media.collegeboard.com/digitalServices/pdf/research/2013/2013-Annual-Participation.pdf

College Board AP Central. (n.d.). *Setting credit and placement policy.* Retrieved from http://apcentral.collegeboard.com/colleges/setting_policy/0,,154-179-0-0,00.html

Delisle, J. R., & Berger, S. (1990). *Underachieving gifted students.* Reston, VA: ERIC Clearinghouse on Disabilities and Gifted Education. (ED321483)

Early Entrance Foundation– The Gifted World. (n.d.). Retrieved from http://www.earlyentrancefoundation.org/giftedworld.html.

Feynman, R. (1985). *Surely you're joking, Mr. Feynman! Adventures of a curious character.* New York, NY: W. W. Norton.

FinAid.org. (n.d.). *No loans for low income students.* Retrieved from http://www.finaid.org/questions/noloansforlowincome.phtml

Frome, P., & Dunham, C. (2002, April). *Influence of school practices on students' academic choices.* Retrieved from http://www.sreb.org/programs/MiddleGrades/publications/reports/Guidance_Research_Brief_4-30-021.pdf

Gross, J. (2002). *Steps to college: The waiting game.* Retrieved from http://www.nacac.com/p&s_steps_0301waiting.html

Guernsey, L. (2005). *College.edu.* Alexandria, VA: Octameron Associates.

Hansen, R. (n.d.). *Are summer college prep or academic enrichment camps right for you?* Retrieved from http://www.quintcareers.com/college_prep_camps.html

Holland, J. L. (1962). Some explorations of a theory of vocational choice: One- and two-year longitudinal studies. *Psychological Monographs, 76*(26, Whole No. 545).

Individuals with Disabilities Education Act, 20 U.S.C. §1401 et seq. (1990).

Johns Hopkins University Center for Talented Youth. (n.d.). *History/mission.* Retrieved from http://www.cty.jhu.edu/about/history.html

Kaufmann, F. (1981). The 1964–1968 presidential scholars: A follow-up study. *Exceptional Children, 48,* 164–169.

Kaufmann, F., Harrel, G., Milam, C. P., Woolverton, N., & Miller, J. (1986). The nature, role, and influence of mentors in the lives of gifted adults. *Journal of Counseling and Development, 64,* 576–578.

Leider, A. (2011). *The A's and B's of academic scholarships.* Alexandria, VA: Octameron Associates.

Leider, A., & Leider, R. (2011). *Don't miss out: The ambitious student's guide to financial aid.* Alexandria, VA: Octameron Associates.

Mathews, J. (2005, November 24). At long last, Advanced Placement is a subject in itself. *The Washington Post Fairfax Extra,* p. VA08.

Mollison, A. (2006). *Surviving a midlife crisis.* Retrieved from http://www.educationnext.org/20061/34.html

National Association for College Admission Counseling. (2001). *Definitions of admission decision options.* Retrieved from http://www.nacacnet.org/research/research-data/nacac-research/Documents/WaitListReport2012.pdf

National Association for College Admission Counseling. (2004a). *State of college admission.* Retrieved from http://www.nacac.com/research_trends.html

National Association for College Admission Counseling. (2004b). *NACAC 2004 early decision/early action guide.* Retrieved from http://www.nacac.com/downloads/04edea_guide.pdf

National Association for College Admission Counseling. (2005). *State of college admission.* Retrieved from http://www.nacacnet.org/MemberPortal/ProfessionalResources/Research/SOCA.htm

National Association for College Admission Counseling. (2012). *NACAC admission trends survey* (Staff report to the NACAC Assembly Wait List Study). Retrieved from http://www.nacacnet.org/research/research-data/nacacresearch/Documents/WaitListReport2012.pdf

National Association for College Admission Counseling. (2013). *Statement of principles of good practice.* Retrieved from http://www.nacacnet.org/about/Governance/Policies/Documents/SPGP_9_2013.pdf

National Collegiate Athletic Association. (2013–2014). *Guide for the college-bound student-athlete.* Indianapolis, IN: Author.

Pappano, L. (2012, November 2). The year of the MOOC. *The New York Times.* Retrieved from http://www.nytimes.com/2012/11/04/education/edlife/massive-open-online-courses-are-multiplying-at-a-rapid-pace.html

Plank, S. B., & Jordan, W. J. (2001). Effects of information, guidance, and actions on postsecondary destinations: A study of talent loss. *American Educational Research Journal, 38,* 947–979.

Princeton Review. (2013). *The Best 378 Colleges, 2014 Edition.* Princeton, NJ: Princeton Review.

Rampell, C. (2013, February 26). Only half of first-time college students graduate in 6 years. *The New York Times.* Retrieved from http://economix.blogs.nytimes.com/2013/02/26/only-half-of-first-time-college-students-graduate-in-6-years/?ref=catherinerampell

Ray, B. D. (2003). *Beyond graduation.* Retrieved from http://www.hslda.org/research/ray2003/Beyond.asp

Reis, S., & McCoach, D. B. (2002). Underachievement in gifted students. In M. Neihart, S. Reis, N. Robinson, & S. Moon (Eds.), *The social and emotional development of gifted children: What do we know?* (pp. 81–90). Waco, TX: Prufrock Press.

Robinson, N., & Davidson Institute for Talent Development. (2005). *Considering the options: A guidebook for investigating early college entrance—Student version* (pp. 31–32). Retrieved

205

from http://print.ditd.org/young_scholars/Guidebooks/YS Guidebook_Early_College_Students_12_08_05.pdf

Roosevelt, E. (1958). *The autobiography of Eleanor Roosevelt*. New York, NY: HarperCollins.

Rudner, L. (1999). *The scholastic achievement of home school students*. Reston, VA: ERIC Clearinghouse on Assessment and Evaluation. (ED435709)

Savingforcollege.com. (n.d.a). *Intro to ESAs (Coverdell education savings accounts)*. Retrieved from http://www.savingforcollege.com/intro_to_esas

Savingforcollege.com. (n.d.b). *Intro to 529s*. Retrieved from http://www.savingforcollege.com/intro_to_529s

Selingo, J. J. (Ed.). (2013). *College (un)bound: The future of higher education and what it means for students*. Boston, MA: Houghton Mifflin Harcourt.

Siegle, D. (2013). *The underachieving gifted child: Recognizing, understanding, and reversing underachievement*. Waco, TX: Prufrock.

Simpson, R. G., & Kaufmann, F. A. (1981). Career education for the gifted. *Journal of Career Education, 8*, 39–45.

Solow, R., & Rhodes, C. (2012). *College at 13: Young, gifted, and purposeful*. Scottsdale, AZ: Great Potential Press.

Springer, S., Reider, J., & Morgan, J. (2013). *Admission matters: What students and parents need to know about getting into college* (3rd ed.). San Francisco, CA: Jossey Bass.

Stengel, R. (2012, October). Reinventing college. *TIME Magazine*. Retrieved from http://nation.time.com/2012/10/18/reinventing-college/

Supplee, P. L. (1990). *Reaching the gifted underachiever*. New York, NY: Teachers College Press.

U.S. Department of Education. (2011). *Digest of education statistics, National Center for Education Statistics*. Retrieved from http://nces.ed.gov/programs/digest/d11/tables/dt11_196.asp

Webb, J. (2013a). *Searching for meaning: idealism, bright minds, disillusionment, and hope*. Tucson, AZ: Great Potential Press.

Webb, J. (2013b, February). *Are we preparing gifted children for college . . . or preparing them for life.* Keynote address presented at the meeting of Our Gifted, Arvada, CO.

Wei, C. C., Berkner, L., He, S., Lew, S., Cominole, M., & Siegel, P. (2009). *2007–08 National Postsecondary Student Aid Study (NPSAS:08): Student financial aid estimates for 2007–08: First look* (NCES 2009-166). Washington, DC: NCES, Institute of Education Sciences (IES), & U.S. Department of Education.

West, T. (1997). *In the mind's eye: Visual thinkers, gifted people with dyslexia and other learning difficulties, computer images and the ironies of creativity.* New York, NY: Prometheus.

Whitmore, J. R. (1980). *Giftedness, conflict, and underachievement.* Boston, MA: Allyn & Bacon.

Willis, G. (2005, August). Saving for college: 5 tips. *CNNMoney.* Retrieved from http://money.cnn.com/2005/08/10/pf/saving/willis_tips/index.htm?cnn=yes

Wrightslaw. (2013). *Twice exceptional children (2e).* Retrieved from http://www.wrightslaw.com/info/2e.index.htm

Wrightslaw. (n.d.). *Special ed advocate newsletter.* Retrieved from http://www.wrightslaw.com/nltr/09/nl.0922.htm

Yermish, A. (2010). *Tips for parents: Cleared for launch—Transition planning for twice-exceptional kids.* Retrieved from http://www.davidsongifted.org/db/Articles_id_10675.aspx

APPENDIX A
Early Entrance College Programs

For the purposes of this book, early entrance college programs are "self-contained." In general, students who attend these schools are developmentally ahead of their age-mates by about 2 years or more. They are ready for college level work at a young age. That does not mean that they are personally ready, so the decision to enroll in an early entrance school should not be taken lightly. The Davidson program offers helpful guidebooks on their websites. There are currently only three programs nationwide that serve groups of children aged 11–15 upon entrance to college. These three programs have specific facilities, support and curriculum geared toward the needs of a group of young scholars, to aid in the transition from what is usually middle school to college (Early Entrance Foundation - The Gifted World, n.d.):

» The University of Washington (Seattle; https://robinsoncenter.uw.edu);

» University of Southern California, Early Entrance Program (http://dornsife.usc.edu/res-honors-faqs); and

» Mary Baldwin College (http://www.mbc.edu/early_college/peg).

Advanced Academy of Georgia

University of West Georgia, Honors House
Carrollton, GA 30118
Phone: 678-839-6249
http://www.advancedacademy.org
The Advanced Academy is a residential, early-entrance-to-college program for gifted and talented high school-aged students. Students generally apply during their sophomore or junior year, but the academy also occasionally accepts younger high-ability students. Students earn concurrent high school and college credit.

Bard College at Simon's Rock

84 Alford Road
Great Barrington, MA 01230
Phone: 413-644-4400
Admission: 800-235-7186
E-mail: admin@simons-rock.edu
http://www.simons-rock.edu
Most applicants are 14 to 16 years old and have completed ninth grade. They earn either an Associate in Arts degree after 2 years or a Bachelor of Arts degree after 4 years.

Boston University Academy

One University Road
Boston, MA 02215
Phone: 617-353-9000
E-mail: academy@buacademy.org
http://www.buacademy.org
A coeducational day school for students in grades 9 through 12. The Academy offers a distinctive curriculum and high school experience for students who are characterized by a love of learning.

The Clarkson School

Clarkson University
8 Clarkson Avenue
Potsdam, NY 13699
Phone: 315-268-4425
http://www.clarkson.edu/tcs

The Clarkson School's Early Admission Program is designed primarily as a one-year residential program for 12th-grade students. Each year, 55 to 80 talented students who have completed 11th grade and have demonstrated high interest and excellence in their academic work are selected for admission. In special cases, students in other grade levels are considered for admission. The Clarkson School community, which includes the Young Scholars Program, provides a strong, supportive environment for students, who live in their own residence hall and enjoy an array of field trips and social activities.

Georgia Academy of Math, Engineering, and Science (G.A.M.E.S.)

Middle Georgia State College
100 College Station Dr.
Macon, GA 31206
Phone: 478-934-3471
http://www.mga.edu/games/

G.A.M.E.S. is designed so that scholastic students can earn both a high school diploma, from their home high school, and an associate degree from Middle Georgia State College simultaneously. Students may also choose to remain at MGSC after high school graduation to earn their bachelor's degree.

Halbert & Nancy Robinson Center for Young Scholars

University of Washington
Guthrie Annex 2, Box 351630
Seattle, WA 98195
Phone: 206-543-4160
E-mail: uwacad@uw.edu

Summer Programs: rcsummer@uw.edu

https://robinsoncenter.uw.edu/

Through early entrance programs, the Robinson Center prepares younger students for college and provides them with challenging, accelerated learning opportunities in a vibrant intellectual community at the University of Washington. Enrichment and summer programs offer classes for highly capable Puget Sound students. Two options are available:

> » The Early Entrance Program provides programs for seventh or eighth grade students.
> » The UW Academy for Young Scholars, the Robinson Center's early university entrance program for 10th grade students, is offered in collaboration with the UW Honors Program.

Missouri Academy of Science, Mathematics and Computing

Northwest Missouri State University

Office of Enrollment

800 University Drive

Maryville, MO 64468

Phone: 877-398-4615

E-mail: MASMC@nwmissouri.edu

http://www.nwmissouri.edu/MASMC

Applicants must be currently enrolled in the 10th grade or its equivalent and must have completed Geometry and Algebra II by the end of their sophomore year. Students attend the Missouri Academy for 2 years, replacing the junior and senior years of traditional high school. While at the Missouri Academy, students are enrolled in a curriculum consisting of all college coursework taught by professors at Northwest Missouri State University. Upon successful completion, students earn an Associate of Science degree as well as a high school diploma.

The National Academy of Arts, Sciences, and Engineering (NAASE)

The Belin-Blank Center for Gifted Education

The University of Iowa

600 Blank Honors Center

Iowa City, IA 52242-0454

Phone: 319-335-6148; 800-336-6463

E-mail: belinblank@uiowa.edu

http://www2.education.uiowa.edu/belinblank/students/naase/

Selected students who have completed coursework equivalent to the junior year in high school may accelerate their academic careers and move into university research and coursework. Academy students are accepted automatically as freshmen into The University of Iowa Honors Program and live together on the honors residence hall floors. The University of Iowa also offers The Iowa Online Advanced Placement Academy for students in grades 9–12.

The Program for the Exceptionally Gifted (PEG)

Mary Baldwin College (women only)

PO Box 1500

Staunton, VA 24402

Phone: 540-887-7039

E-mail: earlycollege@mbc.edu

http://www.mbc.edu/early_college/peg

The Program for the Exceptionally Gifted offers young, academically talented women between the ages of 13 and 15 the opportunity to complete college during their high school years while living in a fully supervised residence hall with their true peers on the campus of Mary Baldwin College. Prospective PEG students are eligible to apply from their eighth-grade year on and are accepted based upon giftedness, consistent academic achievement, and personal maturity. In addition to PEG, Early College Academy is home to an early college program for gifted students 16 or 17 years of age who can choose to complete high school degree requirements in tandem with college courses.

Texas Academy of Leadership in the Humanities (TAHL)

Lamar University
P.O. Box 10062
Beaumont, TX 77710-0062
Phone: 409-839-2995
E-mail: texas.academy@lamar.edu
http://dept.lamar.edu/taolith
The Texas Academy for Leadership in the Humanities is a 2-year residential honors program that allows juniors and seniors in high school to complete their last 2 years of high school credits and their first 2 years of college requirements concurrently, while taking only college courses. This means that a student completes the program with a high school diploma and 60 or more college hours. With Advanced Placement exams and course opportunities, it is possible for students to graduate from high school with even more college hours.

Texas Academy of Mathematics and Science (TAMS)

University of North Texas
TAMS – Sage
1155 Union Circle #305309
Denton, TX 76203-5017
Phone: 800-241-TAMS
E-mail: tamsadmissions@unt.edu
http://www.tams.unt.edu
The Texas Academy of Mathematics and Science is a residential program for high-school-aged Texas students who are high achievers and interested in mathematics and science and have completed 10th grade. While living on campus, students in this 2-year program complete a rigorous academic curriculum of college coursework at the University of North Texas (UNT). Upon completion, students receive a special high school diploma and are classified as college juniors.

University of Southern California Early Entrance Program (EEP)

University of Southern California
Resident Honors Program
3454 Trousdale Parkway, CAS 200
Los Angeles, CA 90089-0153
Phone: 213-740-2961; 800-USC-2961
E-mail: residenthonors@dornsife.usc.edu
http://dornsife.usc.edu/res-honors-faqs/
The Resident Honors Program at the University of Southern California is a one-year early-entrance program for students who have exhausted high school curricula and are capable of college-level work. Students earn a high school diploma while concurrently enrolled in USC classes.

Appendix B
College Planning Web Resources

Acceleration

A Nation Deceived: How Schools Hold Back America's Brightest Students
http://www.accelerationinstitute.org/nation_deceived
A Nation Deceived highlights disparities between the research on acceleration and the educational beliefs and practices that often run contrary to the research.

Career Interests

Career Development Manual–Centre for Career Action
https://emanual.uwaterloo.ca/login_new.aspx

The Princeton Review Career Quiz
http://www.princetonreview.com/career-quiz-overview.aspx

What Can I Do With This Major?
http://www.acu.edu/campusoffices/careercenter/what-can/
http://www.myplan.com/majors/what-to-do-with-a-major.php

College Finding/Planning Internet Sites

Campus Tours (virtual tour guide)
http://www.campustours.com

eCampusTours.com
http//www.ecampustours.com

College Board
http://www.collegeboard.com

College Connections
http://www.college-connections.com

College Navigator
http://nces.ed.gov/collegenavigator
Find colleges based on location, programs, tuition, distance learning, evening courses, and more. Compare up to four colleges. Sponsored by the U.S. Department of Education.

Historically Black Colleges and Universities
http://hbcu-levers.blogspot.com/p/gateway-to-hbcus.html
Gateway to information about Historically Black Colleges and Universities (HBCUs)—where they are located, data and publications, research and development, organizations, and more.

My College Guide
http://www.mycollegeguide.org

The National Association for College Admission Counseling (NACAC)
http://www.nacacnet.org

Peterson's
http://www.petersons.com

Princeton Review
http://www.princetonreview.com

StudentsReview
http://www.studentsreview.com

The University of Texas List of U.S. Universities and Community Colleges
http://www.utexas.edu/world/univ

U.S. News & World Report School Rankings
http://www.usnews.com/usnews/edu/college/rankings/rankindex_brief.php

University and College Directory
http://www.university-directory.org

Financial Aid and Scholarships

College Board Scholarship Search
https://bigfuture.collegeboard.org/scholarship-search
Find scholarships, other financial aid, and internships. Scholarship information is based on the College Board's Annual Survey of Financial Aid Programs.

CollegeNet
http://www.collegenet.com/elect/app/app
Search engines for scholarships and college.

College Scholarships
http://www.collegescholarships.org
Students with disabilities qualify for a number of unique scholarships. As you piece together your college funding package, consider each of the groups you belong to as possible sources of aid. For example, if you are a minority student with a disability studying technology at a U.S. college, each of these unique per-

sonal characteristics—or any combination of them—might open financial aid doors for you.

Fastweb
http://www.fastweb.com
Fastweb is a comprehensive scholarship site that sends you e-mail when new scholarships come up.

Federal Pell Grant Program
http://www.ed.gov/programs/fpg
The Federal Pell Grant Program provides need-based grants to students in postsecondary education.

Federal Student Aid Gateway
http://federalstudentaid.ed.gov
The Federal Student Aid Gateway site offers information, guidance, and tools.

Federal Supplemental Educational Opportunity Grant (FSEOG) Program
http://www2.ed.gov/programs/fseog/
The FSEOG Program provides need-based grants to low-income undergraduate students.

Federal Work-Study Program
http://www2.ed.gov/programs/fws/index.html
The Federal Work-Study (FWS) Program provides funds to students through part-time employment.

The Financial Aid Information Page
http://www.finaid.org

FindTuition.com
http://www.findtuition.com/tp2/ft/home.do

The Gifted Homeschoolers Forum

http://giftedhomeschoolers.org

The Gifted Homeschoolers Forum supports gifted homeschoolers in the United States and around the world through education, advocacy, community, and support.

HowToGetIn.com by Edvisors

http://www.howtogetin.com/

A comprehensive college search by states or regions. Refine your choice by tuition range, campus size, and student population. Features include several handy strategic checklists and calendars you can use as cues for action (dates for tests, etc.).

The Illinois Student Assistance Commission

http://www.isac.org/

The National Center for Learning Disabilities: Teens & Transition

http://www.ncld.org/parents-child-disabilities/teens/scholar ships-for-students-with-learning-disabilities

This website maintains a list of organizations offering scholarships to students with learning disabilities.

Rise Scholarship Foundation, Inc.

http://risescholarshipfoundation.org/

This is a nonprofit resource and scholarship opportunity for high school students who learn differently.

Robert C. Byrd Honors Scholarship Program

http://www.ed.gov/programs/iduesbyrd/index.html

Sallie Mae College Answer

http://www.collegeanswer.com/index.jsp

College Answer is an offshoot of Sallie Mae and has a lot of information for college bound students.

Scholarships.com
http://www.scholarships.com
This website offers lists of scholarships by genre, including scholarships for students with disabilities. Recruitment efforts and financial aid opportunities aimed at students with disabilities now exist at a number of schools. This website offers a searchable database by type of disability.

Smarter Schooling
http://www.smarterschooling.com

SuperCollege
http://www.supercollege.com

U.S. Department of Education Office of Federal Student Aid
http://www.ed.gov/about/offices/list/fsa

Homeschooling Resources

College Confidential: Discussions on Homeschooling and College
http://talk.collegeconfidential.com/home-schooling-college

Home School Legal Defense Association
http://www.hslda.org

Colleges That Admit Homeschoolers
http://learninfreedom.org/colleges_4_hmsc.html

Colleges With Homeschool Admission Policies Online
http://homeschooling.gomilpitas.com/olderkids/CollegeHSpages.htm

Test Preparation

ACT
http://www.act.org/aap

College Board SAT Practice
http://sat.collegeboard.org/practice

College Board Essay Scoring
http://sat.collegeboard.org/scores/sat-essay-scoring-guide

Educational Testing Service (ETS)
http://www.ets.org

Kaplan Education Center
http://www.kaptest.com

Majortests.com
http://www.majortests.com
This website helps students with college entrance exams.

March 2 Success
https://www.march2success.com
March 2 Success was developed as a free, no-obligation tool to help anyone improve their test scores in the areas of English, math, and science. It is particularly useful for international students.

The National Center for Fair and Open Testing
http://www.fairtest.org
This website maintains a list of more than 850 4-year colleges and universities nationwide that admit a substantial number of bachelor degree students without regard to SAT or ACT scores.

The New SAT: Power Tactics
http://www.sparknotes.com/testprep/newsat/powertactics

Study Skills

Center for Advancement of Learning at Muskingum
http://muskingum.edu/home/cal

Study Guides and Strategies
http://www.studygs.net

Talent Searches

Center for Talent Development at Northwestern University
http://www.ctd.northwestern.edu

The Institute for the Development of Gifted Education
http://www.du.edu/idge/giftedness/resources.html

Johns Hopkins Center for Talented Youth
http://cty.jhu.edu

Talent Identification Program at Duke University
http://www.tip.duke.edu

About the Author

Sandra L. Berger has been a citizen activist and advocate for gifted children for more than 30 years. She originally was led down this path by her own gifted youngsters. Berger holds a master's degree in gifted education curriculum and instruction with training in counseling. For 15 years, she was the gifted education information specialist at the ERIC Clearinghouse on Disabilities and Gifted Education and the AskERIC system, responding to thousands of questions about gifted and special education. For more than 15 years, she was a member of the editorial advisory board and a technology columnist for *Understanding Our Gifted*. She has authored numerous articles in the field of gifted education and shares her views on college planning and gifted education through participation in national, regional, and state conferences. Berger and her husband of 54 years currently have 5 grandchildren.

4722
college guides